COLLECTION MANAGEMENT

MEAN
GIRLS
AT WORK

MEAN GIRLS AT WORK

How to Stay Professional when Things Get Personal

Katherine Crowley
Kathi Elster

 New York   Chicago   San Francisco   Lisbon   London   Madrid   Mexico City
Milan   New Delhi   San Juan   Seoul   Singapore   Sydney   Toronto

The McGraw·Hill Companies

1 2 3 4 5 6 7 8 9 0   DOC/DOC   1 8 7 6 5 4 3 2

ISBN   978-0-07-180204-8
MHID   0-07-180204-5

e-ISBN   978-0-07-180205-5
e-MHID   0-07-180205-3

Photo on page 188 by Roberta Raeburn

McGraw-Hill books are available at special quantity discounts to use as premiums and sales promotions or for use in corporate training programs. To contact a representative, please e-mail us at bulksales@mcgraw-hill.com.

This book is printed on acid-free paper.

Library of Congress Cataloging-in-Publication Data

Crowley, Katherine.
Mean girls at work : how to stay professional when things get personal / Katherine Crowley and Kathi Elster.
     p.   cm.
  ISBN-13: 978-0-07-180204-8 (alk. paper)
  ISBN-10: 0-07-180204-5 (alk. paper)
1. Psychology, Industrial. 2. Interpersonal relations. 3. Interpersonal communication. 4. Conflict management. I. Elster, Kathi. II. Title.
  HF5548.8.C683 2013
  650.1'3—dc23
                                       2012032965

650.1

To Carol Crowley,

with love

CONTENTS

CHAPTER 5
Doesn't Mean to Be Mean

ACKNOWLEDGMENTS

There are so many people who have **supported** us along the way, but a few special people stand out. We'd like to **acknowledge** them here.

First, we are extremely grateful to all of the women whom we interviewed (anonymously). **Thank you** for giving us your time and for sharing your honest stories. Without your true experiences, *Mean Girls at Work* would not be possible.

Thank you to our company team for assisting us with this project: Denyse Thompson, Christine Medina, Christine Zarett, and Deborah Brozina.

Sincere **thanks** to the people who pointed us in the right direction for this book: Lea Brunson, Mark Chimsky, Niki Papadopoulos, Elaine Markson, and Gary Johnson.

Without the extra **support** that our families provided throughout the process of writing *Mean Girls at Work*, we could not have stayed sane. **Thank you** to David Winkler for always reading whatever we wrote. **Thank you** Nicole Winkler, for your true belief in us. **Thank you** Clif Eddens, for hot meals and constant encouragement.

Finally, we'd like to express special **thanks** to the McGraw-Hill team. We appreciate your excitement and your belief in our work: Stephanie Frerich, Pamela Peterson, and Sara Hendricksen.

INTRODUCTION

WOMAN-TO-WOMAN RELATIONSHIPS ARE NATURALLY INTENSE. When they're good, they're very good; when they're bad, they can be horrible. The purpose of this book is to give women the knowledge and skills that they need in order to stay professional no matter how other women behave at work.

Our mission is to empower women to support one another in the workplace. Our hope is that anyone who reads this book will gain a greater understanding of how to transform any difficult woman-to-woman relationship into an association that benefits and supports both parties.

Why is it important for women to work well together now? With unprecedented access to education, training, professional opportunities, and buying power, women are positioned to dissolve and move beyond any barriers that previously thwarted their advancement.

The problem is that few women can move up the ranks of their professions if their female colleagues covertly (or overtly) hold them back. While it's natural to assume that most women support other women and want them to succeed, that's not always the case. In fact, studies show that many women believe it is their female associates who are most threatened by the prospect of a woman in power.

By writing *Mean Girls at Work,* we're starting the conversation that many women are reluctant to have. Until recently, most discussions about mean girls in the workplace have taken place behind closed doors or in the company ladies' room. Why? We think it's because, having struggled and fought to gain ground as participants and earners equal to men, women are hesitant to talk about the dark side of woman-to-woman relationships. It feels like a betrayal of the sisterhood. And in fact, women did have to bond together to voice their concerns and establish their legal, political, and economic rights.

This is the next level of feminism. It's time to take an honest look at how we treat one another in the workplace and strive for greater professionalism and support for one another.

Why We Wrote This Book

After the national and international success of our two books, *Working with You Is Killing Me* and *Working for You Isn't Working for Me*, we became known as workplace relationship experts. One day, the training director of a major corporation asked us to give a lecture on "women haters." At the time, we didn't know what a women hater was. The training director explained that women haters were the women at work who were mean to other women.

We balked at the assignment, but we understood that this major corporation must be on to something. So, we asked for a few days to conduct our own research. After polling a few of our clients, we began to realize that this request tapped into an unspoken issue in the workplace—women covertly competing with other women.

We came up with an hour-long lecture that we delivered to a room full of transfixed professional women. As presenters, we knew that we'd hit a nerve. However, while we sensed that this material could be helpful to a wider audience, we also hesitated. Our own protective feelings toward women made it difficult for us to pursue a book that would uncover the unseemly side of feminine behavior.

As authors who write about workplace relationships, we've learned that whenever we write a book, it forces us to examine our own behavior. With *Mean Girls at Work*, we had to take a hard look at ourselves. Where had we been mean, covertly competitive, or indirectly aggressive with the women in our lives? We also revisited those situations in which other women had consciously or unconsciously been mean to us.

Our research included hundreds of interviews with women in more than 20 industries who offered their own experiences concerning woman-to-woman relationships that they'd found difficult, confusing, or just plain hurtful. We are grateful for their candor, their willingness to be vulnerable, and their honest appraisal of what went wrong.

Who Needs This Book

Mean Girls at Work is designed for women entering the workplace who find themselves surprised and perhaps disappointed with one or more of their relationships with a female coworker. It's also intended for women who've been in the workplace for a while and have had great working relationships with women in the past but currently find that they're caught in a power struggle with another woman. In addition, this book can help women in management or human resources who would like a better grasp on how to handle woman-to-woman conflicts. It also has the ability to show women how they may be hurting others without even knowing it, and help them to change their behavior.

How to Read This Book

We've broken down problematic woman-to-woman relationships into seven categories of "mean." We start with the most extreme (meanest of the mean) and go on through varying degrees of potentially mean behavior that you might encounter at work.

In each chapter we describe specific scenarios in which one woman does or says something that feels mean to the woman on the receiving end. We'll tell you what she does, how you feel, what not to do, what to do, and what actions you can take in the future to put the relationship on a professional track.

You may be surprised that we've included a category called "brings out your mean." That's because we wanted to explore the kinds of women whom you may be less than friendly toward, and offer concrete methods for treating those irritating women in a professional manner.

We suggest that you read *Mean Girls at Work* twice. First, use it as a reference book, seeking solutions to your immediate relationship problems. Next, go back and read each chapter to better inform and prepare yourself for all kinds of interpersonal experiences that may arise involving female clients, coworkers, vendors, and bosses. The ideas and suggestions in *Mean Girls at Work* can even be applied to your personal life as well.

We truly believe that girls and women rock! The female wiring that gives us creativity, collaboration, the ability to connect, the desire to nurture, and a strong sense of personal responsibility is ushering in a new world of work. We offer this book as a tool kit that will increase your personal and professional awareness. As you move your career forward, *Mean Girls at Work* can provide real relief for any woman-to-woman relationship that is currently causing you pain.

MEAN GIRLS AT WORK

CHAPTER 1

The Different
Faces of Mean

What Is a Mean Girl?

When you think of a mean girl at work, what comes to mind? Do images of Miranda Priestly from *The Devil Wears Prada* pop into your head? Do you envision Cruella de Vil of *101 Dalmatians* or the Wicked Witch of the West in *The Wizard of Oz*? Do you picture a woman who is unkind, spiteful, vicious, unfriendly, cold, aggressive, manipulative, nasty, vengeful, and power-hungry?

The mean girls (and women) we read about, see portrayed on the screen, and sometimes encounter at work usually share certain characteristics:

- They are the workplace bullies.
- They pick on women who are weaker than they are.
- They say cruel things that make other women cry.
- They freeze other women out.

- They seem determined to take other women down.
- They're jealous of anyone else's success.

These are some of the typical characteristics that emerge when women describe truly unkind women at work. They depict mean girls in the extreme. "Vicious," "cruel," and "vengeful"—such behaviors are easy to recognize and associate with the mean girl profile. A woman who treats her colleagues in such obviously uncaring ways is clearly mean.

But consider the more subtle kinds of mean behavior that one woman can show toward another, the less obvious ways in which one woman might hurt, insult, or otherwise injure her workplace colleagues:

- Have you ever rolled your eyes when a woman you didn't like started speaking?
- Have you ever given or received an intimidating up-and-down scan that said, "I'm judging you"?
- Have you ever gossiped about someone who rubbed you the wrong way?
- Who hasn't watched one woman open her mouth and utter the universally recognizable "agh" sigh of disgust aimed at another woman in a group?

These kinds of mean gestures are harder to detect, yet they are frequently made by women in the workplace. And while you may be a generally kind and loving person, we bet there are certain women you've encountered who bring out your meaner side.

Just as there's a little bad in every boy, there's a little mean in every girl. "Mean" is the inherently female way of showing displeasure, of staking out our territory and telling another woman to back off.

Make no mistake: we are *huge* fans of women. We are women ourselves, and we're invested in the notion that women can and should be full players at work and in the world. We're also aware that woman-to-woman relationships are naturally intense. The biological imperative that compels us to "tend and befriend" can generate amazing friendships and incredibly productive work teams in any setting.

But women are complicated. While most of us want to be kind and nurturing, we struggle with our darker side—feelings of jealousy, envy, and competition. While men tend to compete in an overt manner—jockeying for position and fighting to be crowned "winners"—women often compete more covertly and behind the scenes. This covert competition and indirect aggression is at the heart of mean behavior among women at work.

Over the course of this book, we are going to give you strategies for handling a wide array of situations with women at work. In each case, one or more of the women involved could be labeled "mean." We're going to teach you our method for staying professional no matter how personally another woman attacks you or hurts your feelings.

To begin our journey, let's look at the seven categories of mean that we'll be addressing in this book. Each category will have its own chapter, in which we'll describe specific situations that you may face involving another woman at work, along with field-tested tactics for keeping the relationship professional no matter what happens. Here we go.

Meanest of the mean. These are the women who feel that they must be mean in order to survive. They view other women as objects to be won over, manipulated, or eliminated. They lack compassion, and they are unable to see anybody else's point of view. An example is the Ice Princess who treats everyone around her with disdain.

Very mean. These women are tough on the outside and insecure on the inside. They do and say mean things whenever they encounter a woman who threatens them. They are quick to feel jealous, envious, and competitive with another woman. An example is the vicious gossip who spreads rumors to make another woman (whom she's jealous of) look bad.

Passively mean. This category of mean girls includes any woman who acts nice, but is covertly competitive. Because she fears confrontation, her mean comes out indirectly—through exclusion, omission, and avoidance. An example is the coworker who "accidentally" excludes you from a meeting where your attendance matters.

Doesn't mean to be mean. These are the women who are extremely self-absorbed. Their unconscious, inconsiderate behavior strikes other women as mean, but they don't see it. They are oblivious to the impact of their actions. An example is the coworker who is chronically late, leaving you in the lurch.

Doesn't know she's mean. These mean girls behave in ways that they *think* improve a situation, but that actually alienate the women around them. They are usually quite self-righteous and controlling. An example is a coworker who bosses you around because she thinks you need the benefit of her knowledge.

Brings out your mean. Certain women at work may get on your nerves. They have poor interpersonal boundaries and demand a lot of attention. Their neediness brings out *your* mean. You find yourself lashing out, gossiping about the person, avoiding her, or making faces when she's speaking. An example is the insecure coworker who asks too many questions, interrupting your workflow and depleting you of your energy.

Group mean. Sometimes mean girls form packs. There's usually a leader who enlists other women to taunt, tease, shut out, or otherwise attack an unsuspecting female employee. An example is a workplace clique that whispers when you walk by; you feel alienated and humiliated by them.

Our "Don't Go There" Process

For every mean girl situation we describe, we're going to show you how to manage the other woman's behavior by using our five-step "Don't Go There" process.

Women are *processors*. Most women sort out their experiences by hashing them out with other women. When something good or bad happens to us, we talk about it. For example, if a woman is bullied by a certain type of mean girl, she may feel attacked. She then seeks out friends, coworkers, family members, or mentors to hear her story, confirm how she's feeling, and offer different ideas for addressing the situation.

When a woman feels attacked, she automatically goes through a three-step process:

1. **She finds an ally and reports (with emotion) what the attacking woman did.**

   Example: "You've got to hear what she just did to me."

2. She follows the report with how she's feeling.

> **Example:** "I'm so mad I could spit. She humiliated me in front of everyone. How could she do that?"

3. She then describes how she'd like to counter-attack

> **Example:** "I'm never talking to her again," or, "The next time she asks for help, she's out of luck."

If the attacked woman acts on her impulse to counterattack, she takes that workplace relationship out of the professional realm and turns it into a personal conflict. Many workplace wars start this way. Harsh words exchanged between two women can lead to a silent war that lasts for months and sometimes years.

Our "Don't Go There" process incorporates this natural flow of events and prevents the incident from turning personal by giving you options. Instead of telling you to counterattack, we say, "Don't go there." We then tell you what you can do to address the mean girl's behavior without losing your professional standing.

Here Is the "Don't Go There" Process

1. *What She Does.* We describe what the mean girl does, such as how she may attack you.

2. *How You Feel.* We define the natural, emotional reactions you're likely to have in response to her behavior.

3. ***Don't Go There.*** We point out what *not* to do by showing you how to avoid counterattacking her. (This is the most difficult step—refraining from both verbal and nonverbal methods of fighting back.)

4. ***Go Here.*** We offer professional, reputation-enhancing, job-saving actions you can take to manage the situation.

5. ***Going Forward.*** We explain how to work with (and protect yourself from) this type of mean girl in the future.

Each chapter contains a number of scenarios, one narrative story called "In Her Own Words," and a few "Coffee Breaks" that give you insight and energy as you discover how to keep interactions with any mean girl professional, no matter what she does.

Need a cup of coffee now? Here's a coffee break that describes the silent weapons that women use to communicate. Read it, and see if you can relate.

Coffee Break

Silent Weapons Women Use

Whoever said, "If looks could kill . . ." must have been referring to a woman. Women are the masters of nonverbal communication. One way in which women can be passively mean is by sending nonverbal messages. Consider whether you've ever received or delivered any of the following:

Up-and-down scan. This "sizes up" another woman and lets her know she's being judged.

Rolling the eyes. This conveys irritation and impatience with whatever the other woman is saying.

Averting her gaze. Avoiding eye contact can say, "I'm mad at you," or, "I want nothing to do with you."

Nudging a girlfriend as another woman walks by. This is usually accompanied by a whisper or a sneer; it lets the other woman know that she's being talked about.

Sighing. This communicates, "Not this again," or, "Are you finished?"

Sneering. As the upper lip curls up, the eyes narrow to let another woman know, "You disgust me."

Giving a disapproving glance. This establishes the fact that one woman is judging another.

Offering a fake smile. This is a mocking gesture that says just the opposite—"I don't like you," or, "I think you're an idiot."

Turning away from her. Usually done as the woman approaches, this gesture lets her know, "I'm not speaking to you."

Talking to the hand. A woman raises her hand up to another woman's face to communicate, "I don't care about you, and I don't want to hear what you have to say."

Shaking the head in disbelief while furrowing the brow and raising the upper lip. This signals, "You've *got* to be kidding me."

Pointing or wagging a finger. This indicates, "You are the problem," or, "I blame you for this."

Each of these gestures is a form of attack. If you've been on the receiving end, you know how humiliating it is to be subjected to one of these assaults. If you've doled out one or more of these gestures, you can increase your professionalism today by deciding to put your nonverbal weapons down.

You are now ready to embark on a journey into the world of *Mean Girls at Work*. We hope you enjoy the ride. Take your time, and remember that staying professional when things get personal takes practice.

CHAPTER 2

Meanest
of the **Mean**

In most cases, it's possible to break a cycle of mean behavior between women and get the relationship to a better place. Then there are the extreme cases. These involve women who see every woman (and some men) as a threat—before they even know her.

These women consider being mean—whether covertly or overtly—to be essential for survival. Unlike the average gal, they can't tolerate a level playing field. In their world, there are only winners and losers, and they need to be on top. We call these women the "meanest girls" because they'll do whatever it takes to win.

While most women have the capacity to behave poorly toward other women on occasion, the meanest girls are fundamentally different. You can never really *win* with these women. For this reason, handling the "meanest girls" at work requires a different strategy.

Let's travel back to grade school or junior high and the first time you encountered a truly mean girl. She may have been the head cheerleader or the leader of a popular clique. Perhaps she was very pretty or supercool and aloof. She may have teased you for being different or made fun of you in front of her friends. She probably excluded you from her lunch table or smirked as you walked down the hall. You may have caught her whispering about you to her girlfriends.

Anyone who was part of her pack had to agree with everything she said, dress according to her style, and follow her orders. Mean girls in the early years are intimidating, belittling, and bullying. Anyone who is subjected to their taunting or teasing behavior feels humiliated and embarrassed. Adolescence and the self-consciousness that comes with it are hard enough. Mean girls can make your teenage life truly awful.

Many women spend their teen years avoiding mean girls. They eventually form their own group of solid friends, and they make sure that they steer clear of the mean girl's venom. They also learn how to protect each other from a possible attack.

If you were lucky enough to navigate the mean girls of grade school, junior high, and high school successfully, it can be shocking when you discover that a grown woman at your dream job is mean, too. At first, you can't believe it. You try everything you know to make things better with this woman—compliment her clothes, bake cookies for her, or help her out when she's in a jam. And still, she's cold and rejecting.

If you're dealing with a truly mean girl, one of her limitations is that she's literally incapable of seeing your point of view. Meanest girls can feel sorry for people who are weaker than they are, but they cannot *empathize* with them. That is, they truly cannot imagine what another person is thinking or feeling. For the meanest girls, other people are objects to be charmed, manipulated, controlled, or eliminated.

Sound harsh? Perhaps. But that's because the meanest girls are missing the usual psychological equipment that most women have. Unlike the majority of women at work, who naturally tend-and-befriend, the meanest girls can't really cooperate. They don't know how to have reciprocal, win/win relationships.

When you're dealing with a meanest girl at work, your goal is not to unite—she's not capable of that. Instead, your aim is to protect yourself and maintain a neutral alliance. What follows are nine of the most common types of meanest girls at work, along with solid strategies for defending yourself against them.

Hang on. Read the profiles in this chapter, and put some of our strategies to work. It may not be easy, but we trust that you can maintain a solid professional demeanor despite the meanest girl's personal assaults.

She's an Ice Princess

What She Does

Sometimes you encounter a female colleague who has an air of superiority toward anyone who is her peer or her subordinate. She carries herself regally. She dresses impeccably. She acts like a princess who can't be bothered with commoners. While she'll put on the charm for anyone who is in a position of authority (her boss, a client, or the CEO), she's cold, dismissive, and demeaning to everyone else.

At first, you may not believe that she's as cold as she appears. You try to connect with her woman to woman. You strike up a conversation looking for some common ground—maybe you admire her outfit or ask about her commute—but she does not take the bait. Instead, she acts disinterested and bored.

When she speaks to you, she acts as if you're below her. At an event, she bosses you around, treating you like her servant. Her disdain for you seems unfounded. Yet it starts to hurt your self-esteem.

How You Feel

Her demeaning behavior makes you feel self-conscious and uncomfortable. You get nervous whenever you have to spend time in her presence. Working with her feels awkward and oppressive. She's so uncooperative that you dread any project that requires her participation.

Don't Go There

- Don't spend your energy agonizing over why she treats you so poorly.
- Don't try to charm her into being nice to you—it won't work.
- Don't cut her out of meetings or projects just to avoid interactions with her.
- Don't call her derogatory names as she leaves the room.

Go Here

This kind of situation is a challenge for any woman. Ice Princesses usually do quite well at work because, while they aren't nice to the people around them, they know how to charm the people above them. And this kind of mean girl does produce results. Your best approach is to keep a cool distance from her while maintaining a professional relationship. Do *not* take her behavior personally. See her as an unpleasant obstacle that you have to deal with, but you do not have to like.

Going Forward

Understand that you may be working for a company that values productivity more than professional courtesy. Many Ice Princesses continue to be rewarded by their employers because they're good at managing the people above them and know how to impress. If your company promotes employees who mistreat and devalue their peers, you may have to decide whether you're in the right corporate culture.

She Sees All Women as Adversaries

What She Does

From the moment you meet her, you get a sense that she's not interested in bonding with you. She may give you "the look," sizing you up as potential competition. She doesn't want to join you for lunch, and she never asks about your life outside of work. Whenever you spend time with her, she seems angry, impatient, and tense. She may casually mention that she's better equipped to do your job than you are. You catch her saying negative things about other women as well. If a female colleague is absent from a meeting, she'll use it as an opportunity to criticize and blame her for something.

Her behavior around men is completely different. She smiles at them, jokes with them, and talks about business with ease. She can hang out in their company for hours. And she never trashes men verbally to get ahead. In fact, she often remarks that she prefers the company of men because, "They're so much simpler to deal with."

How You Feel

Spending time in this person's company is a prickly experience. You feel uncomfortable and unwelcome. You sense that she dislikes you, but you don't understand what you did to alienate her. When she looks you up and down or frowns as you're talking, you get a sinking feeling that she'd like to take you down.

Don't Go There

- Don't work overtime to win her over by being supernice.
- Don't confront her.
- Don't write her off as "silly" or unimportant.
- Don't talk to the other women about what a witch she is.

Go Here

You are in the grip of a supercompetitive woman who views every other woman as a rival. Your best bet is to try diffusing her killer instinct by letting her know that you aren't a threat. You can do this by appreciating her work ("Great presentation"), noticing her expertise ("No one knows financial analysis like you do"), and complimenting the way she handles certain business situations ("You handled that client like a pro").

Going Forward

You'll want to keep a cool distance from this person and never be lulled into the illusion that she is on your side. Her competitive, combative behavior is not personal. You haven't done anything wrong to warrant her antagonistic opinion of you (and all other women). She simply cannot experience female coworkers as anything other than obstacles in her path.

She Puts You Down Publicly

What She Does

It could be about what you're wearing, the project you're working on, or your personality. You could be walking into a room, attending a meeting via Skype, or just about to give a presentation. This type of female colleague says derogatory things to you in front of your peers: "Didn't you take any English courses in college? This document is a mess." "I'd save that outfit for casual Fridays." "Why don't *you* talk to the client? You're good at pretending you care."

How You Feel

You feel sideswiped and shocked. You weren't expecting to be attacked, and you're not sure what you did to deserve such treatment. Physically, you feel a flush of heat go through your body as your heart races. You may have a queasy feeling in your stomach. Embarrassed, angry, and hurt, you either shut down or want to fight back.

Don't Go There

- Don't react out of anger—you'll probably say something that will make the situation worse.
- Don't give yourself a hard time for not speaking up in the moment.
- Don't retell the story ad nauseam to anyone who will listen.
- Don't say to others, "You're not going to believe what she said to me. . . ."

Go Here

After this kind of experience, we suggest that you start by taking steps to purge the emotional toxins that naturally emerge from receiving her verbal jabs. You could engage in rigorous exercise after work, get a massage, or try some other form of self-care. If you need support, seek out the counsel of a trusted workplace confidante—a mentor or seasoned professional. Explain what happened, and ask for advice: "What is the best way to handle this kind of situation?"

Going Forward

With time and practice, you'll be able to address your colleague's comments without feeding into her cattiness. Regarding the messy document, you could say, "Thank you for the feedback. Yes, I did take English classes in college, and I did very well. I'll make all the corrections you suggested." In response to the "casual Fridays" comment about your outfit, you could say, "Thanks for the feedback. It's important to know how others perceive me." And to the coworker who compliments your ability to "pretend to care," you can respond to her dig lightly with a simple, "Thank you."

Coffee Break

How to Take a Mean Girl's Behavior Less Personally

A common question that you may ask yourself if a mean girl targets you is, "What did I do to deserve this treatment?" It's natural to think that there must be something specific about you—something you're doing or saying—that's triggering her vicious behavior. The truth is that it's not really about you. Even though her words and actions seem very personal, you aren't the first person she's gone after, and you won't be the last.

It is extremely important that you find ways to not take her mean words to heart. One way to depersonalize a mean girl situation is to look at the facts. Ask yourself the following questions:

1. Does this mean girl have a history of conflict with other women who've preceded you? (Ask someone who's been at your company for a long time to validate this.)
2. Does she have a reputation as being "someone to avoid"?
3. Do you notice other women giving you sympathetic looks when she attacks you?

A "yes" answer to any of these questions is a sure sign that you are just one of a long line of targets. Unfortunately, your mean colleague simply can't be nice to others. You need to know that you are not the cause of her malicious tactics. See her as someone who is sick and suffering, and do your best to stay out of harm's way.

She Gives Harsh and Demeaning Feedback

What She Does

There are some female colleagues who deliver feedback in a way that cuts you to the core. If you come to her with a question, she may say, "Don't waste my time with stupid questions. Figure it out on your own." As you're explaining the details of a project, she interrupts you and says, "Get to the point. You're too boring to listen to." After you give a presentation to the boss, she whispers, "That was awful. You'd better update your résumé."

How You Feel

Her words stun and confuse you. You feel hurt, insulted, and embarrassed. You may want to lash back, but you're not sure how to do so.

Don't Go There

- Don't get defensive and fight back.
- Don't run around saying, "Can you believe what she just said to me?"
- Don't let her see you crying or getting upset.

Go Here

First and foremost, do *not* take her remarks personally. This is an angry individual who is using you as her current target. You are not the first person to feel her verbal barbs, and you won't be the last. Having said that, you can take one of two approaches:

1. Disarm her by using humor or a neutral response. If you're going for levity, you can say something like, "You say the sweetest things." If you want to stay neutral, simply say, "Thanks for the feedback."

2. Ignore her. When she says something harsh, don't respond at all, and don't show (with your face or body posture) that she's hurt you.

Going Forward

Clearly, this is not someone whom you want to have in your inner circle. At the same time, you do want to establish a courteous, unemotional relationship with her. The less you react to this person's harsh feedback, the less interesting you will be as a target. To calm yourself down and rid yourself of her negative energy, you may need to engage in some form of regular exercise. Negative people like this exude toxic energy, and you'll want to purge the anger she causes you from your system.

She's Extremely Argumentative

What She Does

There's a woman at the office who seems compelled to argue with everything you say. When you're in a meeting, she challenges every statement you make. On conference calls, she disagrees with your point of view. If you work together on a team, she corrects you at every turn. Even during a casual lunch conversation, she disputes your opinion about a movie that you both watched.

How You Feel

Working with a person of this kind is extremely frustrating. You don't understand what you've done to warrant her constant aggression. It feels unfair and hurtful. When she starts to challenge you, you feel attacked. You're stunned and confused—why is this happening?

Don't Go There

- Don't fight back—stooping to her level will make you look bad.
- Don't bad-mouth her to your boss (or anyone else).
- Don't solicit the support of your colleagues against her.

• Don't be overly nice, hoping that she won't challenge you (it won't work).

Go Here

Approach your colleague and ask to have a private conversation with her. Let her know that you respect her opinion and you want to work with her but that she seems to have a problem working with you. You'd like to talk about it. See what she says. If this woman denies that there is a problem, say, "Okay. If you decide there's something you want to tell me, I'm available."

Going Forward

The next time your colleague challenges you, instead of defending yourself, take a moment to hear her out. After she speaks, say, "I respect your opinion. Thank you." Then move on. Often this kind of person wants to be heard and feels competitive toward you. If an opportunity arises, you could also put her in charge of an area that she feels strongly about. This will give her positive attention and reduce her focus on you.

She Solicits Personal Information and Uses It Against You

What She Does

This kind of colleague is extremely crafty and difficult to detect. Her attitude is one of friendly concern as she shows interest in you. She always asks how you are doing, and she's very interested in your life outside of work. She seems like a safe confidante because she shares some of her issues with you as well—whether they involve weight and dieting, relationships, or financial woes.

You leave meetings with her feeling warm and cozy. You often wonder whether you've shared too much. You may find yourself talking about your health concerns, an addiction you're struggling with, or your spouse's career stress. Conversations with her feel less like business meetings and more like therapy sessions.

Trouble starts when you realize that the private information you've shared with this woman has become public—hurting your reputation at work. A colleague, boss, or client expresses interest in one of the confidential topics you've discussed only with her.

The person may say, "Has your husband found a job yet?" or, "I heard you might lose your home." In addition, your confidante hangs out some of your personal laundry for others to see. At a meeting, she might innocently ask, "Are you keeping up with your AA meetings?" or, "You look stressed. More problems at home?"

How You Feel

Once you realize that your colleague is using your personal information to damage your professional standing, you feel betrayed, blindsided, and ambushed. You're angry and indignant that she took advantage of you. When you're interacting with your peers at work, you feel self-conscious and embarrassed—like a loser. Since you're aware that others know a great deal about your personal affairs, you feel vulnerable to more attacks. Your head spins, and you wonder what else she is saying and who else she is informing.

Don't Go There

- Don't bother confronting her—she'll deny her wrongdoing.
- Don't spread rumors about her in retaliation—it will backfire.
- Don't freeze her out.

Go Here

Once you become aware of this woman's game, stop playing it. Do not confide any more personal information to her. When she invites you to sit down and chat, keep all the conversation focused on work. If she asks you about private matters, say, "I appreciate your concern, but I'm good." If she inquires about someone else's personal problems, say, "I wouldn't know." If she tries to reel you in by divulging the personal struggles of a mutual colleague, find a way to excuse yourself as soon as possible or simply steer the conversation back to work.

Going Forward

Keep a cool distance from this person. Maintain a courteous exterior, but do not let her rope you into her web. If you like, warn others of her manipulative ways by saying, "Be very careful of what you say around her. She's not good at keeping confidences."

Coffee Break

You Don't Have to Suffer Alone—When to Reach Out for Professional Help

Dealing with a "meanest girl" can do a number on your psyche. Her harsh treatment may crush your self-confidence, ruin your mood, or damage your health. If you find yourself dreading work, having difficulty getting out of bed, crying throughout the day, or abusing alcohol or prescription drugs, we encourage you to seek professional support.

You can hire a psychotherapist, a career counselor, or an executive coach. The important thing is that this individual understands the psychological challenges of the workplace—including woman-to-woman relationships in which one woman acts in cruel and callous ways toward another.

You may want to ask your HR department for a referral. Or you can tap into your network of friends and see if one of them can offer a qualified expert. Perhaps your spiritual community has resources available for guidance as well.

The point is that you don't have to suffer alone. Short-term help can provide a safe place where you can relieve stress and acquire the interpersonal skills necessary to manage this extreme situation.

She's Cold and Rejecting

What She Does

She's the one person in the office who consistently seems to freeze you out. When you walk into the office and say hello to her, she offers a cool "hello," and then turns away. When you ask her how her weekend was, she answers with one word, "Fine." Whenever you try to join a conversation that she's participating in, she walks away.

How You Feel

You feel rejected—as if you've done something wrong. But no one is telling you what your offense was. You start to question yourself. You become self-conscious and uncomfortable whenever you are around this person. You wish someone would tell you what's going on.

Don't Go There

- Don't beat yourself up or assume that you must have done something terribly wrong to deserve her chilly treatment.
- Don't retaliate by being cold back to her.
- Don't bad-mouth her to other women.

Go Here

This kind of icy behavior usually emerges when you represent something negative to the offending party. It may be that you are from a different race, a different religion, or a different socioeconomic class. It could be related to your age, your appearance, or your credentials. Whatever the issue is, your frosty coworker isn't responding to *you*, she's responding to what she thinks you stand for.

As upsetting as it is to be unfairly judged, you will not be able to change this woman's mind about you. To manage this relationship, you have to work very hard at remaining courteous, kind, and professional. Deliver whatever work product you must to this individual, but don't expect a friendly reception.

Going Forward

Make sure that you spend plenty of time with the people who *are* able to treat you with warmth and respect. Understand that anyone who has to freeze another person out probably has a very defensive and insecure point of view. Refrain from trying to win over your cold colleague. Instead, focus on doing your best work, remaining civil, and letting her chilly behavior roll off your back.

IN HER OWN WORDS

She Sabotages You

It's 8 A.M. on Monday morning. Carrie, the top salesperson for her company, arrives for her weekly meeting with the sales manager. As she walks into his office, she's surprised to find him frowning. "I'm afraid you're slipping, Carrie," he says. "You aren't giving our customers the degree of service they need."

Carrie is stunned. "What do you mean?" she asks.

"Your number one account has requested Marlene as the point person, and I have to give it to her," he replies.

Carrie is crestfallen. She's always had a great relationship with this client, and her boss has always praised her performance. This sudden change doesn't make sense to her. She goes to Jo (another salesperson) for advice.

"I don't understand what just happened," she confides to her friend. "I just lost my best account to Marlene."

Jo looks up from her computer, "That's interesting, because I saw Marlene having lunch with your number one account last week. Did you know about that?"

Carrie's heart starts to race, "No, I didn't," she says.

"I'm afraid sweet-talking Marlene is out to steal your clients," Jo says.

Carrie challenges Jo's hypothesis. "But that's impossible," she argues. "Marlene has always complimented me, and admired my work; she acts like my best buddy."

Jo nods. "Exactly. Let me tell you how a saboteur works." Carrie takes a seat, and Jo begins to explain: "To your face, saboteurs are overly solicitous. They compliment you on your appearance, your intelligence, and the way you present yourself. They convince you that they want to be your friend. They act as if you are their idol."

"That's exactly what she's done," Carrie says.

"But, behind your back," Jo continues, "saboteurs are delivering a very different message. Carefully and subtly, they say things that slowly erode your reputation. They have a knack for relaying untrue statements about their targets to other people." Carrie begins to feel anxious. "Over time," Jo says, "they infiltrate your core business relationships—with clients, coworkers, and authority figures. Their goal is to take these connections away from you."

Carrie realizes that Jo is right. Marlene is trying to sabotage her. "Oh my God, what a mess! What do I do now?" Carrie implores.

"Don't worry," Jo assures her. "You can repair this situation. The key is to appear cool and act strategically. Don't yell at her for stealing your client. And don't run around maligning her to everyone else."

"But what about *my* reputation?" Carrie asks.

"Well, you've got a few things to do," Jo then instructs Carrie. "First, go to Marlene and calmly say, 'I know exactly what you're doing, and it's not going to work.' She will act as if she doesn't know what you're talking about, but the message will register.

"Next, I want you to mount an aggressive outreach campaign to all of your clients. Reinstate yourself as their primary contact. You'll probably discover that Marlene has already misrepresented you in several instances, but this will be an opportunity to clear up those misunderstandings."

"I can do all of these things," Carrie responds. "But what if I see Marlene encroaching on someone else's territory?"

"Well," Jo pauses, "I would suggest approaching that person and giving her a warning. You can say, 'I suggest you protect your business relationships around Marlene.' If that woman wants to know more, you can share your experience in a factual, professional way."

"You mean, I should explain that I worked with Marlene, became friendly with her, and then lost my top client to her?" Carrie asks.

"Exactly. No editorial remarks. Just the facts."

She Wants to Get Rid of You Because You're Different

What She Does

It could involve race, religion, political affiliation, or ethnicity. It could be because of your age, your accent, your weight, or your sexual orientation.

Whatever the "difference" is between you and your coworker, your very presence threatens her. At meetings, she glares at you. She has probably held back in some way from the beginning. When you were introduced to each other, for example, she acted as if shaking your hand might give her a contagious disease.

She shames you in small and consistent ways. If you're running late, she's at your desk keeping time. If you have trouble performing any task, she jumps on it with glee. She may comment, "I just wonder if you have the skills necessary for this job."

She looks for opportunities to ridicule the things about you that *are* different. If your attire is different from hers, she may say, "Is that your native costume?" If you observe a religious holiday, she'll put it down by asking, "Is that for real, or did you make it up?" Should your political views differ significantly from hers, she may say, "Do you really consider yourself an American?" If you are heavier than she is, she may zero in on your food choices and say, "Do you really need that?"

How You Feel

Working with this kind of person is *extremely* painful. Her behavior is mean, humiliating, and insulting. Her attempts at intimidating you cut to the core of your self-esteem. You feel stunned, confused, and helpless. You don't know how to defend yourself against this self-appointed vigilante. You have revenge fantasies that include her getting hit by a truck or being hauled away by the police.

Don't Go There

- Don't avoid her.
- Don't become passive-aggressive by cutting her out of communications.
- Don't cop an attitude and answer every question with a snide remark.
- Don't rant about her on Facebook, Twitter, or any other social media forum.

Go Here

As difficult as this may be, your best approach in this very uncomfortable situation is to address your colleague directly. You aren't looking for her to become your friend. You are simply stating what your experience is and bringing her mean, aggressive behavior out into the open.

The goal is to clear the air—if possible. Try saying, "It seems that you don't like me, and I want to find a way that we can work together. We don't have to be friends, but we do have to work with each other. Can we agree on that?" See how your colleague responds.

Going Forward

Dealing with this extremely uncomfortable situation is inherently unfair. Despite your best efforts, short-term justice may not be attainable. It's unfortunate that this person is so closed-minded and fearful that she cannot see beyond her prejudices.

One thing you can do is document her behavior. Keep a running list of what she does, noting the time, the date, and the specific words exchanged between the two of you. If her cruel and demeaning behavior continues, you may need to go to Human Resources and report your experience. In the long run, you may want to simply find a better situation.

She Hacks into Your Private Communications (Twitter, Facebook, and E-mail), Then Uses Them Against You

What She Does

It begins innocently enough. You join a new company and, eager to forge new relationships, you add certain coworkers to your Facebook and Twitter accounts. One day, Human

Resources calls you in for a meeting. You learn that your office neighbor (a woman you thought had befriended you) has printed out your personal posts and highlighted any remarks that could be interpreted as controversial. You also discover that she convinced the department's IT person to hack into your company e-mail account searching for more incriminating evidence against you. HR gives you an official warning, reminding you that using company property for personal purposes is not acceptable and that saying anything that could hurt the company's image will not be tolerated.

How You Feel

You feel completely and utterly betrayed and violated. You're shocked and in disbelief. You're also humiliated and embarrassed. You may want to scream at your invasive, disrespectful colleague.

Don't Go There

- Don't go back onto your Facebook and Twitter accounts and blast her.
- Don't start printing out posts from *her* social media accounts.
- Don't plant a virus in her computer.

Go Here

If you want to keep your job, you'll have to clean up your social media accounts. Remove any videos, quotes, photos, or political statements that could be viewed as offensive. (You can decide later whether you find that degree of self-censorship too compromising.) Next, approach your coworker for a brief conversation. Let her know that you've made some adjustments to your social media accounts. Also tell her that you wish she'd felt comfortable enough to address her concerns about your posts in person, rather than going immediately to HR. You could say, "In the future, if you have a problem with anything I do or say, please come to me first."

Going Forward

Someone who acts this covertly is not likely to confront you on any matter. For your own protection, quietly block her from your social media accounts. Consider this a tough lesson in professional development. In many cases, the freedom of expression that you enjoyed in earlier years must be curtailed to fit the requirements of your professional life.

Coffee Break

Developing Your Mean Girl Detector (Mean-o-Reader)

The pain of working with one of these meanest girls has one clear reward:

> You can use your hard-won experience to detect and avoid working with truly mean girls in the future.

Before taking that new job or joining a different department, make sure to investigate whether there are any meanest girls lurking (working) there.

Remember:

- Meanest girls are usually hard to connect with.

- They often act cold and aloof.

- They give off a tense energy—people around them seem nervous and on edge.

- They are described as "difficult to work with but valuable to the company."

- They exhibit a superior attitude toward others.

- They appear unfriendly.

If you detect these qualities in a soon-to-be coworker, you have a decision to make: either you go in with your eyes wide open and use the techniques you've learned to manage the relationship or you look for other opportunities (and healthier companies).

JUST BETWEEN US GIRLS

If you are contending with a "meanest of the mean" girl, you are in the triathlon of difficult workplace relationships. Interacting with this brand of woman requires a great deal of energy, perseverance, and internal strength. It's easy to crack under the pressure of handling her negative energy and toxic barbs every day.

Here are three things to remember:

1. *Stay in good mental shape.* Make sure you have safe confidantes and a solid support system around you.

2. *Don't let her live in your head.* This kind of woman can occupy your mind and dominate your conversations outside of work. You'll need to make a conscious effort to clear your mind and refrain from talking about her after work hours.

3. *Be kind to yourself.* It's natural to look for relief from a "meanest of the mean" girl by turning to junk food, late-night TV, bottles of wine, or online shopping. We encourage you to trade in these quick fixes (which will make you feel worse the next morning) for healthier, kinder methods of self-care. Exercise, a good night's sleep, or going to the movies, the theater, or a museum with friends can lift your spirits and restore your energy so that you can be your best professional self despite the mean girl's behavior.

CHAPTER 3

Very
Mean

C ertain women at work have a gift for turning any professional situation into a personal attack. Their words are like weapons. They can make you blush, perspire, flinch, or even cry. You aren't sure what you've done to warrant their wrath, but you seem to be a target. These are the women we call "very mean."

Very mean girls do and say mean things whenever they encounter a woman who triggers feelings of insecurity in them. A very mean girl may feel insecure about her looks, her intelligence, her likability, or her pedigree. She may have a chip on her shoulder because she didn't grow up in the right neighborhood or attend the right college. Perhaps she has an older sister who won all the awards and garnered all the praise. For whatever reason, she's operating from an internal deficit.

Very mean girls are quick to feel jealous, envious, and competitive with other women. Unlike the meanest girls, who have a hard time feeling genuine affection for other women, very mean girls can bond with some of their female colleagues. They tend to like women who are either equal to or below them in status.

Some very mean girls will decide you're a threat the minute they see you. Others will interrogate you about your background and your upbringing in an attempt to establish where you stand in their pecking order. For example, if a very mean girl asks where you went to college and your school seems more prestigious than hers, that could trigger her jealousy. Or, if she notices that you carry a designer handbag, she may ask where you got it. She's listening for signs of wealth that she may not have.

Once a very mean girl perceives you as a threat, she begins her attack. She may gossip about you, belittle your accomplishments, talk down to you, or aggressively disagree with you. Fielding her attacks is emotionally exhausting and takes a toll on your confidence. Her negativity toward you is very painful.

You may find yourself rehearsing and rehashing conversations with this woman. You may incessantly talk about her with your friends outside of work. You may stay up at night worrying about her next mean moves. It's common to have revenge fantasies in which you throw hot coffee on her white dress or she gets transferred to Siberia.

Personal Strategies for Coping with Mean Girls

Before we address specific very mean girl situations, we want to give you some personal strategies for taking care of yourself:

1. Get Physical

When you're dealing with a very mean girl, it's easy to absorb her negative energy. Her actions also generate feelings of hurt, anger, anxiety, and frustration inside you. We believe that the best method of purging this toxic energy is exercise.

If you're an athlete, you understand this. You know the benefits of working out—the natural mood elevators that are available through regular physical activity. If you're not someone who exercises on a regular basis, now is the perfect time to consider inserting some form of fitness activity into your schedule. You may want to sign up for a zumba class, make a running date with a friend, or return to a sport (such as tennis, swimming, or biking) that you used to enjoy.

The important thing is to get your body moving so that you can release your tension and feel better. If you can work out physically, it will improve your mood and allow your mind to see the problem in a different light. No matter what she does during the day, a very mean girl won't have the same grip on you after you engage in rigorous physical activity.

2. Get Support

Just as we are strong proponents of exercise to release negative energy, we encourage you to seek emotional support outside of your company to help you navigate this relationship. You may want to investigate short-term counseling or engage the services of a career coach.

One of the best forms of support is a professional mentor. This should be a woman who is older than you are—someone who's has accrued enough work and life experience to recognize what you're going through. Mentors are better than peers in these circumstances because they are emotionally removed from the situation and may have previous experience with similar cases. You can tell a mentor what the mean girl does, and she'll help you find a professional solution to your personal nightmare.

Now we're ready to dive into the specific types of very mean girls that you may be dealing with at work. Brace yourself. We know these scenarios aren't pretty. Still, if you're currently caught in one of these situations, we can help.

IN HER OWN WORDS

She's a Vicious Gossip

Ellie, the assistant to the VP of operations, can't wait to accompany Leila to the coffee truck. As soon as they arrive downstairs, Ellie pulls Leila aside and says, "I think one of your very good friends is on the chopping block. Her head's about to roll."

Alarmed at the news, Leila asks, "Who are you talking about?"

Ellie smiles and says, "Your buddy Sue down in Marketing. But you didn't hear it from me." On that note, Ellie laughs and walks away.

For the next week, Leila walks around in a state of anxiety. Her friend Sue is on vacation, and Leila doesn't want to ruin her time away. At the end of the week, Leila approaches Ellie for verification. "Are you sure it's Susan who's going to get the axe?"

Ellie shrugs her shoulders and says, "Oh. Maybe I was wrong."

The next week, as staff members gather for a departmental meeting, Leila watches Ellie go after Jake. "He's late again," she complains. "I bet he's putting extra time in at home so his wife won't suspect he's having an affair."

One employee takes the bait. "Who's he having an affair with?"

Ellie responds, "The new receptionist. Isn't it obvious?"

Leila is now both disgusted with and afraid of Ellie. She sees how malicious Ellie's words are, and she wonders what mean-spirited rumors Ellie may be circulating about her. Working around someone this vindictive makes Leila anxious and upset.

Leila contacts Gail, a former boss who's always willing to act as her informal mentor. She describes the situation, and Gail immediately gets the picture. "I've seen this before. You're dealing with a vicious gossip. It's always unfortunate when a company keeps someone like this despite her lack of discretion." Gail explains that employees like Ellie tear people down in order to feel better about their own lives. "If you ask your coworkers about Ellie, you'll find that her longtime colleagues take everything she says with a grain of salt."

"But she shouldn't be allowed to get away with spreading false rumors," Leila protests.

"What makes you think she does get away with it?" Gail responds. "I'll bet she hasn't been promoted in years."

Gail then gives Leila specific instructions for how to handle Ellie. "The next time she approaches you with a juicy piece of gossip, act as if you aren't interested. Look at your watch, yawn, or interrupt her by saying, 'I'm sorry, but I have to go. Catch you later.'" Gail adds, "If you're in a meeting and she dishes out a rumor involving a coworker's personal life, don't engage."

"I think I can do that," Leila says. "Do you have any more suggestions?"

"Yes," Gail says. "Focus on treating Ellie in a cordial, professional manner. And don't ever share information about another person when she's in the room."

She Belittles Your Accomplishments

What She Does

Just as you accomplish something to be proud of, there's someone in the office who makes it her job to denigrate your success. You are delighted to receive an industry award, but your happiness quickly cools when your colleague says, "Congratulations, but you know that's not a very prestigious award." Or, after you land a major account with a prominent company, your colleague says, "I've worked with them before. Good luck meeting their standards." Or, when you complete certification in a work-related program, she says, "Wow. That was fast. They must have lowered their requirements."

How You Feel

Your colleague's verbal jabs feel like psychological punches in the stomach. When she first delivers her message, you feel stunned and confused. Her remarks may shake your confidence and leave you feeling unworthy. On the other hand, her words may also infuriate you, triggering an intense desire to strike back.

Don't Go There

- Don't let your snippy coworker's comments bring you down.
- Don't believe that her devaluing remarks lessen your accomplishments.
- Don't waste your energy defending yourself.
- Don't attack her back.

Go Here

Whenever this coworker belittles your accomplishments, do your best not to react. You can say, "Sorry you feel that way." Then walk away. What you need to understand about this person is that she is belittling you in order to feel better about herself. Her unsupportive comments reveal more about her own insecurities and her feelings of inadequacy. She literally does not believe that there's enough success to go around.

Going Forward

Remember that this is someone who can't be happy for you. You need to realize that you are not the first woman she's been jealous of, and you won't be the last. You'll probably catch her devaluing someone else's accomplishments in the near future. Keep a cool, professional distance in dealing with her. Be friendly without becoming friends.

She Tells Lies About You to Others

What She Does

You notice that one of your solid professional relationships has suddenly eroded, and you don't know why. It could be a formerly friendly coworker in another department who now avoids you, a client who becomes curt and dismissive toward you, or a professional colleague who clearly has false information about you.

Perhaps a cubicle mate approaches you and whispers, "You're still here? Sally said you hated this place." Or, another colleague comes up and says, "Sally told me you're not carrying your weight on that big project." Or, a well-intentioned workplace friend asks, "Is it true that Sally had to rewrite your report because you completely botched it?"

You start to realize that Sally is destroying your reputation by telling lies about you and that the damage is spreading.

How You Feel

When you first realize that someone is spreading lies about you, you're mortified. Your heart races, your stomach drops, and you may want to throw up. You can't believe that this is happening to you. You also can't believe that your colleagues are buying into her fabrications. After the initial shock passes, you become hurt and enraged. You also worry about the damage that's already been done.

Don't Go There

- Don't become hysterical and run around saying, "I can't believe this is happening!"

- Don't counterattack by making up lies about her.
- Don't enroll your girlfriends to attack her as a group.
- Don't go to your boss and accuse your colleague of defaming your character.

Go Here

A woman who tells lies about you is trying to tarnish your reputation in an attempt to improve her own. She believes that the only way to get ahead is by eliminating the competition. You could consider her sabotaging behavior a form of flattery—she perceives you as a winner who must be toppled.

If you can, it's best to go directly to your lying colleague and let her know that you're onto her game. Say, "I've heard some untrue things that you've said about me. I'd like you to stop." Being the coward that she is, she's likely to deny any wrongdoing or claim that her statements were misinterpreted. Her response doesn't really matter. Once she knows you're aware of her tactics, she will most likely stop.

Going Forward

To counteract any damage your colleague may have done, you must now wage your own public relations campaign. That means that you should approach anyone whom you suspect your lying colleague misinformed and say, "I've learned that you may have heard some false information about me, and I'd like to clear up any misunderstandings." If there's a specific lie that you'd like to correct (for example, that you botched an important report), look for opportunities to tell the truth about the situation.

If you suspect that your lying coworker is determined to continue her mudslinging campaign, make sure you insinuate yourself into any meeting, business function, or e-mail chain where she might attempt to do more damage. Also ask your colleagues to be on the lookout.

Coffee Break

Why Some Women Cannot Admit to Their Bad Behavior

This may be hard to believe, but some women literally are psychologically incapable of admitting that they've done something wrong. If you've come across a coworker of this kind, you know what we're talking about. Even if you present her with the facts about an error she made, she'll squirm and try to deny it. If you insist that she apologize for something mean that she said or did, she'll refuse and try to pin the blame on someone else.

What's going on?

When an individual continually refuses to take responsibility for her actions, you're probably bumping up against a structural problem. That is, her internal hard-wiring makes her incapable of true self-reflection. While she may appear to be cocky and arrogant, her identity is actually on shaky ground. She can't admit to wrongdoing because psychologically she can't tolerate the notion of being at fault.

We know that this concept is hard for you to fathom. You can't imagine why a woman wouldn't take responsibility for her own conduct. You're probably quick to admit your mistakes; you're eager to apologize if you sense that your actions or words may have offended another woman. But the truth is that not all women are designed the same way.

If you find yourself working with a woman who can't own up to her mistakes or missteps, you may never have the satisfaction of hearing her say, "I'm sorry," "That was my fault," or, "I can see your point." You may simply have to consider her psychologically handicapped and move on.

She Speaks as if You Aren't in the Room

What She Does

You are in a planning meeting with two colleagues. When the subject of a report you've been working on comes up, one of your coworkers turns to the other and says, "I'm not sure what she's doing, but that report had better be done on time."

Or, you're in the ladies' room and your coworker sees that you're wearing jeans. Instead of addressing you, she turns to her girlfriend standing next to her and says, "Are we allowed to wear jeans on a Monday?"

Or, you're part of a work group that's meeting for the first time. As you sit down to join the group, one woman turns to another and says, "Who assigned her to this team?"

How You Feel

You are shocked by the brazen attitude and behavior of this woman. You can't believe that she just spoke to a mutual colleague as if you weren't in the room. You feel unfairly attacked. Your face heats up as a flash of anger surges through your body. You don't know whether to wring her neck or cry.

Don't Go There

- Don't stand up and walk out of the room.
- Don't retaliate by cursing at her.
- Don't say, " I'm obviously not welcome here."
- Don't rush back to your desk and unfriend her on Facebook.

Go Here

Take a few deep breaths, try to calm your system down, and realize that your colleague is angry with you for some reason. Instead of stomping out or attacking back, respond to her calmly and directly. Ask, "Have I done something to offend you?" If she says, "No," continue to address the topic at hand. "If you're concerned about my report," you can say, "I assure you that I'll have it done. Maybe you and I can talk about this in private later." To address the jeans issue, you can say, "If you want to know why I'm wearing jeans, it's because my department is going on a field trip today." To clarify why you were assigned to a particular work group, explain, "My supervisor assigned me to this group because I bring database expertise that this project really needs."

Going Forward

Understand that this person probably feels intimidated by you. While this may be hard to comprehend, her behavior is a defensive response to you. It may be your looks, your education, your enthusiasm for the job, or the fact that you are well liked. Something about you triggers her jealousy, and she feels the need to put you down.

Going forward, your best policy is to disarm this easily threatened colleague by giving her the respect and attention that she craves. Acting friendlier and more interested in this mean girl may go against your instincts, but trust us on this one.

She Publicly Makes Fun of Something You Confided to Her

What She Does

You're in a staff meeting, and there's a heated discussion about e-mail protocol. "E-mail shouldn't be used to replace important conversations that we should be having in person," you argue. "Yeah," your coworker pipes in, "like your boyfriend should have called you instead of ending the relationship with an e-mail, right?" She smiles and winks as she says it.

How You Feel

You're totally embarrassed and humiliated. Your private life has just been exposed, and you are mortified. You can't believe your colleague just broke your confidence in an open meeting.

Don't Go There

- Though it may be tempting, try not to glare in disbelief.
- Don't retaliate by sharing a personal painful secret of hers with the staff.
- Don't text another friend to berate your clueless colleague.
- Don't accidentally trip her as she's walking out of the room.

Go Here

Say, "I think we have enough examples right here at work that we don't have to bring up my personal life." Then take a few breaths to cool your system down and continue participating in the meeting.

Going Forward

After the meeting, arrange to speak privately with this colleague to let her know that her comment was hurtful. Make a mental note to stop confiding any personal information to her. You can continue to be friendly without getting too close. Even if your coworker apologizes for her remark, she may not have the discretion to keep confidences.

She Has a Negative Reaction when You Receive Praise

What She Does

You get promoted, win an award, or receive public acknowledgment from your company CEO. Full of excitement, you're shocked when one of your workplace friends reacts to your good news negatively.

When the boss announces your promotion, you seek out your girlfriend, expecting her to share your exciting moment. After two texts, an e-mail, and a call, you realize that she's not responding. When you catch her trying to pull out of the company parking lot without being seen, you know she's avoiding you.

Or, the CEO publicly recognizes you for a job well done, and you leave the conference room elated. You're surprised when your good friend says nothing about the acknowledgment. Instead, she says, "Wow. That was boring. What are we having for lunch?"

How You Feel

You feel confused and deflated. You don't understand why this person isn't happy for you. You wonder what you did to deserve that kind of treatment. Her negative reaction makes you question the value of your accomplishments. You start to play down your successes.

Don't Go There

- Don't let your colleague's jealous reaction spoil your success.
- Don't assume that you did something wrong.
- Don't ask this person why she's not happy for you.

Go Here

Connect with the people who have proven to be supportive to you in the past, and share your good news with them. Realize that your workplace friend's negative reaction is teaching you about her—she may be highly competitive and have difficulty with anyone outshining her. Disarm this competitive colleague by continuing to build her up and sharing the credit for anything that you achieve.

Going Forward

It's important to understand that as long as you don't threaten this kind of coworker, she can cooperate and collaborate with you. Just be aware that she is limited. She may be incapable of being happy for other women unless she is in a superior position.

She Talks Down to You

What She Does

You may have a colleague who addresses you in a way that always feels condescending. It seems that she thinks you aren't very smart. If you ask her a question, she sighs, rolls her eyes, and says, "Let me see if I can put it in words simple enough for you to understand." When you propose a new solution to an old problem, she immediately says, "We already thought of that." Every time you offer your opinion, she says, "That's nice. Let's move on."

How You Feel

You leave interactions with this person feeling embarrassed, belittled, and misunderstood. Part of you wonders, "What's wrong with me?" You start to question your intelligence, and your confidence gets shaky. You may also feel furious and indignant that this woman treats you in such a disrespectful manner.

Don't Go Thère

- Don't get defensive with this person.
- Don't turn to your colleagues and say, "Did you hear what she just said?"
- Don't attack her verbally.
- Don't run to other people for protection.

Go Here

Arrange a meeting with this woman and try to set things straight. In private, ask her if there's something you've done to offend her that's resulted in her addressing you in a condescending manner. If she denies that there's a problem, give her concrete examples of the patronizing statements she's made. In some cases, your colleague may apologize and refrain from talking down to you in the future.

Going Forward

Women who talk down to other women are usually angry and covertly competitive. The most important thing to understand is that everyone can see through her petty behavior, and no one buys into her assessment of you. The next time she talks down to you, stop, take a breath, and move on. Act as if her remarks have absolutely no impact on you. The better you get at not reacting to her, the less likely she is to keep sparring.

Your best revenge is to do well and forge relationships with other people who are in positions to further your career.

Coffee Break

Don't Forget to Breathe

Whenever you're in a stressful situation, you can experience immediate relief by focusing on your breath—inhaling and exhaling. Gentle deep breathing calms the mind and soothes the body. It takes only a moment, but you have to remember to do it. Try this simple exercise:

- Inhale slowly and deeply as you silently count to three: "1, 2, 3."

- Hold your breath for the count of three: "1, 2, 3."

- Exhale slowly and deeply as you silently count to six: "1, 2, 3, 4, 5, 6."

Repeat this practice at least three times. Then check your body and see how you feel. Are you more relaxed? Do the exercise three more times to get the full effect.

Now, the next time you're engaged in a heated conversation or someone behaves in a way you don't like, take a few gentle deep breaths—inhaling, holding it, and exhaling—until you feel yourself calming down. The best part is that no one will even know you're doing it!

She Praises You Publicly but Puts You Down Privately

What She Does

Certain women limit their covertly competitive behavior to behind closed doors. In public forums, they're courteous, appreciative, and positive. In private, the claws come out. When you're both attending a large staff meeting, you find yourself sitting alone with her during the break. She turns to you and says, "I notice your input isn't very well thought out." At another time, you're in the elevator together, and she says, "You might want to hire an image consultant to improve your professional appearance." After a very positive meeting with several departments, she finds you in the ladies' room and murmurs, "I didn't think your report was as good as everyone else seemed to."

How You Feel

Her words make you feel sick inside. Your stomach may churn; your shoulders may get tight. You may feel a flash of heat rise through your body. You may feel hurt, but you may also feel indignant. Whatever good feelings you had prior to her comments are completely wiped out. You feel attacked and wounded.

Don't Go There

- Don't attack back.
- Don't go to your boss and say, "You'll never believe what _____ just said to me."
- Don't take her cutting words to heart.

Go Here

Understand that any woman who engages in this type of activity is unhappy herself and jealous of you. Once you really understand that the words come from an envious place, you can start to distance yourself from the message and the messenger.

Going Forward

Avoid any situations that put the two of you in a closed setting. Should she make overtures about you joining her for lunch or a social event, politely refuse.

She's Extremely Friendly, Then Extremely Cold

What She Does

Sometimes a close workplace friendship can turn sour very unexpectedly. The association starts out on a very high note—she's extremely friendly and interested in you during the early phase of your relationship. You become close buddies and trusted confidantes. If she goes for a break, she asks you to join her. If you're both in a meeting, she sits by your side. She's always ready to go out to lunch or to hang out after work and chat. Over time, you become very close. You develop shared jokes and know how to make each other laugh during stressful moments. You feel a sense of community with this person. Seeing her face always brightens your day.

Then, something happens. It may coincide with a change in status. One of you may be promoted or transferred to another department, or perhaps you simply don't see each other as often. All you know is that your colleague suddenly goes from hot and interested to cold and distant. Her previously warm and engaging attitude becomes disengaged and even hostile. She may stop returning your e-mails, ignore your text messages, and disregard your phone calls. She may be too busy to have lunch with you, or she may make a date with you, only to stand you up.

You sense that she's avoiding you, but you aren't sure why. The more you pursue this former workplace friend, the cooler she behaves in your presence. Even more upsetting, your cool colleague may turn her attention and interest toward someone else.

How You Feel

You feel displaced and replaced. You experience a mixture of sadness, anger, confusion, and hurt. Her sudden change of heart makes no sense to you. You don't know what you did to cause such an extreme negative reaction on her part. You also feel the loss of a friendship that previously meant a lot to you.

Don't Go There

- Don't waste your time trying to win her back.
- Don't assume that you did something terribly wrong that alienated her.
- Don't wear down your friends by insisting that they explain what happened.

Go Here

When a workplace friend suddenly turns cold, there's usually very little you can do to alter the situation. You could approach your former friend and ask if there's something that you did that pushed her away. Say, "Your friendship means a lot to me. Is there any way we can repair this?" If she says yes, you're in luck. Be open to hearing what she has to say. If, on the other hand, she continues to stonewall you, then your only choice is to move on.

Going Forward

Sudden breakdowns of intense workplace associations are painful to endure. You may have to grieve for the loss before you can truly move on. You need to know that this type of individual does well only during the early phases of a relationship. She cannot sustain closeness—even though her initial behavior seems very warm and real. Over time, you will discover additional casualties of this hot/cold coworker; women who were also initially drawn in as a best workplace friend, only to be frozen out weeks later.

She Constantly Disagrees with You in Public

What She Does

It happens every time you're in a meeting with her. You make a comment, and she immediately contradicts what you're saying. She begins her statements with, "I disagree," or, "That's not right," and then goes on to do her best to prove you wrong. If you are both meeting with someone in authority, she quickly interrupts you with a contrary point of view. She'll correct you in an e-mail chain and question your findings in a report. She seems determined to oppose you and to make you look bad.

How You Feel

Initially, you are startled by her constant negative reaction to you. Her comments feel aggressive, unfounded, and personal. You can't understand why she is compelled to oppose you at every turn. You wonder what you did to deserve this treatment.

Don't Go There

- Don't interrupt her in midsentence and ask, "What did I do to deserve this treatment?"
- Don't attack back, saying, "No, you're wrong!"
- Don't go to the boss and complain about her.

Go Here

Try this: the next time your coworker contradicts what you're saying in public, deflect it. Say, "That's a good point. Let me incorporate it with what I'm saying." Sometimes giving a woman like this credit for her ideas takes the edge off her competitive jabbing. If deflection doesn't work, you may have to approach her privately and ask, "Is there something I'm doing that bothers you?" If she's self-aware, your question may help her see what she's doing.

Going Forward

This kind of situation is difficult, but you can continue to take the high road by thanking your contradicting colleague for her input and acknowledging her opposing point of view. Trust that you are not the only one who notices her combative, petty behavior. Take her need to shoot you down as a compliment of sorts. You threaten her, which means that she sees that you have talent. Keep moving forward with your own career.

She Can't Forgive a Mistake You Made

What She Does

There may be certain situations in which you make a mistake and your colleague can't get over it. Perhaps you're giving a PowerPoint presentation together, and you mistakenly bring the wrong file. Or you're both working toward a deadline, and you unintentionally deliver your part late—making her look bad. Or you plan a business lunch, and you book it at a steakhouse when she's a vegetarian. Perhaps you have one drink too many at the company holiday party and you accidentally share her relationship problems with your boss.

You know that your colleague can't forgive you after one of these transgressions because her attitude toward you goes from friendly to frozen. No matter how many times you apologize, she remains as cold as ice. She may give you a limp smile after you swear that it will never happen again, but she never gives you a second chance. From that day forward, she keeps her distance, branding you as unreliable, unprofessional, inconsiderate, or whatever judgment she establishes about you as a result of that single incident.

How You Feel

You feel embarrassed and ashamed of the mistake, but also totally frustrated because she's written you off based on one professional slipup. You feel guilty for displeasing her and anxious for her to move forward. You are angry that she won't give you the opportunity to rectify her impression of you.

Don't Go There

- Don't apologize to her over and over again for the same thing.
- Don't justify your behavior and vilify her to your friends.
- Don't spend hours replaying the mistake in your head.
- Don't retaliate by freezing her out.

Go Here

Believe it or not, your first job in this situation is to forgive yourself for whatever mistake you made. As long as you hold yourself culpable, her vindictive, unsympathetic attitude will continue to hurt and haunt you. Mistakes should be used as vehicles for learning—not as a reason for permanent punishment. You need to understand that you did not intend to harm your coworker, make a vow not to make the same mistake twice, and move on. As for your colleague, your best bet is to treat her professionally and ignore her spiteful behavior.

Going Forward

Unfortunately, for this kind of person, holding grudges and resentments is a way of life. Trust that her unforgiving attitude is not about you, even if you erred to her detriment. Over time, you will see that you're in good company—as others make professional errors around this person, they will join you in the penalty box.

Coffee Break

Could You Drop a Pound of Resentment?

> *Resentment is like swallowing poison and waiting*
> *for the other person to die.*   —MALACHY MCCOURT

Resentment is a dangerous emotional weapon. Resentments usually develop when someone hurts, disappoints, or angers us. If a coworker hurts your feelings by saying something insensitive, you may resent her and ignore her at work. If a colleague drops the ball during an important project, you may hold a grudge against her from that day forward.

While it's natural to use resentment as protection from further hurt or disappointment, it doesn't really help. Resentment doesn't feel good inside, and it never improves a workplace relationship. Harboring resentment keeps you stuck in emotional negativity and forces you to operate from a defensive position.

It's OK to remember what happened, but it's more important to move on.

If you find yourself feeling resentful toward another woman, tell yourself to let it go now and replace your negative thoughts about her with something positive.

You can protect yourself from a woman who is insensitive, selfish, or mean-spirited without regurgitating bitter thoughts and feelings about her. Letting go of resentment isn't easy, but it is possible. Practice releasing one of your resentments today.

Drop a pound of resentment and see how much lighter you feel.

She Agrees to Back You, but Doesn't

What She Does

You both have a complaint to lodge. You even meet together to discuss it. You've agreed that there's power in numbers, so you commit to broaching the subject together. It could be a policy that needs to change, a disruptive coworker who should be disciplined, or a supervisor who acts in an offensive manner.

You schedule a meeting with the boss to discuss the issue. You confer with your colleague and determine your strategy. Once the meeting begins, however, something happens. You launch the discussion by presenting the problem to your boss. The boss then turns to your colleague and asks whether she agrees with your assessment. She says, "Actually, I don't have a problem with this situation."

How You Feel

You're shocked and embarrassed; you can't believe that your colleague just changed her story and hung you out to dry. You are angry and disappointed. You feel set up and disgusted. After all the planning that went into presenting this issue, she turned on you in front of the boss.

Don't Go There

- Don't confront your colleague in the meeting, telling her she's a liar.
- Don't stare at her viciously for the rest of the meeting.
- Don't leave the meeting and alert everyone you know of her horrible behavior.
- Don't shut her out and give her the silent treatment.

Go Here

As soon as possible (later that day or the next day), ask to speak with her. You can meet face to face or have a scheduled phone call. (Do not leave this conversation to text, Facebook, Twitter, or e-mail.) When you have your conversation, be direct. Say, "We had an agreement to back each other. What happened that you changed your mind? And why didn't you tell me before the meeting?"

Let your coworker answer these questions.

Going Forward

Because this woman has broken the trust between you, you must now proceed with caution. Understand that, for whatever reason, this individual was not able to take a stand with you. (It's likely that she's uncomfortable taking a stand in her own life as well.) Maintain a professional, cordial attitude, but do not bring her along on any more encounters where you need someone to back you.

JUST BETWEEN US GIRLS

If you are the target of a very mean girl's envy or wrath, you've had to weather a number of personal attacks on your character. Your greatest challenge is to resist taking her words and actions to heart. Very mean girls can make the women they go after feel stupid, incompetent, uninformed, or unworthy. Battling their negative messages takes work and practice. Here are our two strongest suggestions.

First, instead of thinking that there must be something wrong with you, look at the very mean girl and understand that she has a problem. Clearly, she is not happy. Chances are that she's not happy with herself, her own life, or her career. There's a saying that, "Hurt people hurt others." This certainly holds true for very mean girls.

Next, take actions to remember your value. Make a list of every employer, every colleague, and every customer with whom you've interacted successfully. Draw on your closest friends and family for reminders of your skills and talents. You may even want to contribute some time to a cause you care about to help rebuild your confidence and feelings of self-worth.

CHAPTER 4

Passively
Mean

A "passively mean" girl is conflicted. On the one hand, she thinks she should be nice. On the other hand, she's deeply competitive. These opposing forces inside her result in passive-aggressive behavior.

If you're working with a passively mean girl, you'll have a hard time pinning her mean actions down. You may think that she intentionally excluded you from a meeting or failed to give you important information, but should you confront her, she'll always deny it. You end up feeling totally frustrated and confused.

Because passively mean girls present such a warm and friendly façade, it takes a while to identify them. Unlike very mean girls and the meanest girls, a passively mean girl will smile when she sees you, treat you cordially in meetings, and even pose as a workplace friend. This feigned friendliness makes it hard for you to imagine that she could be doing unfriendly things behind your back.

The key to handling a passively mean girl at work is to trust your gut. In other words, you must tune into your intuition or trust your feelings when bad things start to happen in situations that involve her.

For example, if you suspect that a coworker intentionally left you out of an important e-mail chain, but she claims that the omission was an innocent mistake, make a mental note to be on the alert. You can accept her apology on the surface, but make a promise to yourself to watch her actions going forward. Trust that if you have a feeling that she's competitive with you, you're probably right.

Another way to uncover a potentially passively mean girl is to heed any warnings from your colleagues. A workplace girl-friend may say, "Just be careful around Diana," or, "Don't get too cozy with Michelle." Someone may forward you an e-mail in which your passively mean coworker describes you in less-than-glowing terms. If others advise you to watch your back around a seemingly lovely woman, listen up and take the hint.

It may be hard to believe that someone who seems very nice doesn't always have the best intentions. You may have to take your nice girl blinders off to manage this kind of colleague effectively. The good news is that once you figure out whom you're dealing with, you can find a way to work around her passive-aggressive behavior.

You Overhear Her Gossiping About You

What She Does

You could be walking by a conference room, passing by someone's cubicle, or standing in a line at Starbucks when you overhear a workplace friend talking about you. She might be repeating something you said, critiquing something you did, or making fun of something you wore. Whatever it is, the message is not kind.

How You Feel

Besides being shocked and hurt by this experience, you'll probably also feel sick inside. Your heart may start racing. You may feel a flush of heat through your body. Most women in this situation feel angry and betrayed.

Don't Go There

- Don't tell her off.
- Don't call another friend and report what just happened.
- Don't shut her out forever for committing the offense.
- Don't run away and hide.

Go Here

First, take time to cool down. Run, walk, swim, take a few deep breaths, or take a relaxing bath—do something to release the negative energy you feel because you heard someone gossip about you. If you need to confide in someone, pick a person who is removed from your work situation—someone who can listen without getting involved.

Next, decide whether you are able to address the gossiper privately. Ideally, you want to approach her and say, "I overheard you talking about me to someone else yesterday. In the future, if you have a problem with my behavior, I'd prefer that you communicate it directly to me." The recipient may deny that she said anything. You can still repeat the message like a mantra: "OK, but in the future, I'd still like you to communicate with me directly."

If this approach seems too confrontational and you need to work your way up to saying something, then stay professional, but don't discuss anything of a personal nature with her.

Going Forward

This is a tough situation; you will naturally feel betrayed by whomever you caught gossiping about you, so rebuilding a working relationship with your colleague will take a while. The key is to keep a cool (but not cold) professional distance and remain cordial in all of your interactions. Do not confide personal information to her, as she cannot be trusted. At the same time, do not shut her out. Think, "friendly but not friends."

Coffee Break

How Gossip Hurts

While it can be tempting and satisfying to gossip about other women at work, it really is a double-edged sword. Professionally, if you're known as a gossip, it can hold you back. You may be viewed as less trustworthy than other professionals and incapable of holding information in confidence. You may also be seen as someone who lacks discretion. At the same time, gossip erodes the reputation of whomever you're talking about.

She Excludes You from a Meeting

What She Does

Someone makes an innocent inquiry: "What time is that planning meeting tomorrow?" or, "See you at tomorrow's conference call," or, "Are you prepared for the client meeting this afternoon?" You suddenly become aware that there is a meeting scheduled concerning a project you're working on, and you haven't been invited.

How You Feel

You get a sinking feeling in your stomach. You feel left out, rejected. You wonder what you did wrong and why the organizer of this meeting didn't invite you. You start to doubt your value and your standing among your peers.

Don't Go There

- Don't assume the worst.
- Don't run around asking other people if they're going to this meeting, making yourself more emotionally upset.

Go Here

Contact the person who planned the meeting directly. Say or write: "I understand there was a meeting planned regarding a project that I'm involved in, and I was not included. I'm assuming that this is an oversight. Is that accurate?" Nine out of ten times, you'll find that it is an oversight. Occasionally, there may be some other reason. If the meeting planner who excluded you says, "I didn't think you had the time to sit in on this meeting," or, "I didn't think it was important to you," respond with, "I do have the time, and I would like to be included in any future meetings of this kind."

Going Forward

If you find yourself being excluded by the same woman over and over again, repeat the process. Each time it happens, reinforce the fact that you would like to be included. Say, "I would like to be included in any future meetings of this kind." Then, let it go. Don't harp on it by recounting the problem to others. And do your best not to obsess about the situation. Instead, apply the energy you would spend worrying to producing stellar results in other areas.

IN HER OWN WORDS

She Excludes You from an Important E-mail

After a lovely evening out with her new boyfriend, Christine gets up feeling delighted and content, until she checks her e-mail. Her friend Sandy has forwarded an e-mail chain concerning a project that Christine has been working on for several weeks. This particular e-mail refers to a significant change in the project's direction that Christine doesn't recognize and wasn't told about.

Christine's heart starts to pound. Her good mood turns into panic. As she scrolls down the e-mail chain,

Christine sees that one of her coworkers, Dee, launched this e-mail chain earlier in the week, informing everyone on the team (except her) about this change. It appears that the entire work team has been in conversation without Christine's input for two days.

As Christine showers, dresses, and puts on her makeup, she can't help feeling outraged and left out. "How could Dee do this to me?" she frets. "Is this going to ruin my reputation with the other members of my team?" At the same time, she's grateful to Sandy for forwarding the e-mail chain.

As she heads out the door for work, Christine sends Sandy a text: "Thanks so much for the heads-up. Can you meet me at the Caffeine Hut before work?" Sandy is quick to respond yes. As Christine enters the café, she spots Sandy sitting at a table with a hot latte for her friend.

"Dee has done this to me before, Christine," Sandy explains. "I didn't handle it well. I confronted her. Dee denied everything and accused me of being paranoid."

Christine nods her head and asks, "Do you think I'm in trouble, though? I'm afraid I might get fired."

"No," Sandy assures her. "You just need to join the conversation."

The two craft a plan. Christine will compose her strategy for the project's new direction in a fresh e-mail and send it out to the team, apologizing for her late comments. Being careful not to blame anyone, she'll tell the team that she needed some time to think about this change and how to incorporate it.

Christine thanks Sandy for her help, and the two agree to watch out for each other whenever it comes to correspondence involving Dee. Christine also decides to pay a friendly visit to the excluding coworker's cubicle. She approaches Dee and says, "I'm sure it wasn't your intention, but you accidentally left me off that e-mail chain concerning the new direction of our project." Dee looks surprised. Christine continues, "Please make sure to include me on all future e-mails."

She Cuts You Out of a Project

What She Does

It happens while you're attending a weekly departmental meeting with your colleagues. There's an audit going on, and you've been playing a major role. As you sit in the meeting, you discover that you've been taken off the project altogether. "We need you for more important things," your female supervisor says. This seems strange to you, especially since you've really enjoyed spearheading this project. You suspect that your supervisor wants you out of the picture so that she can take credit for the end result.

How You Feel

Deprived of the opportunity to complete a project you care about, you feel sideswiped, confused, and cheated. It seems unfair to be robbed of work you enjoy. You feel angry that you won't get credit for your efforts. You may want to yell at your supervisor or get her fired.

Don't Go There

- Don't storm out of the meeting in a huff.
- Don't quietly go on strike because you feel cheated.
- Don't talk to all of your colleagues about how unfair this situation is.
- Don't assume that you did something wrong to deserve this.

Go Here

Your best recourse is to cool off and then take action. Cool off by taking a brisk walk outside the office, washing your face with cold water, or drafting an angry e-mail that you never send. Once you've purged the negative feelings, you can craft a document that calmly lays out the practical reasons why you would like to continue working on this project. You can send this document to your supervisor, with the understanding that if she still wants you off the project, you'll have to comply.

Going Forward

You may be working for someone who wants to hold you back because you don't fit the mold or because she doesn't like your style. If this is the case, you may want to explore other job options. In the meantime, see if you can uncover the kind of work style your supervisor prefers. Schedule a meeting with her and ask, "Is there something I could have done differently on this project so that I could have continued working on it?" If your supervisor says yes, take notes and try to follow her lead.

She Fails to Give You Important Information

What She Does

You're working on a project with another woman. Your boss informs her that the deadline has been moved up. The boss asks her to inform you, and she never does. You discover this unsettling fact 10 minutes before an important meeting at which that same boss is expecting to see a final draft. At that moment, your colleague remarks, "Did I remember to tell you that our project is due today? I finished the graphics. Do you have the copy?" Shocked by this disconcerting news, you say, "Why didn't you tell me?" "I'm sorry," she quips, "You weren't around when the boss came by. I tried to find you. Then it must have slipped my mind."

How You Feel

You feel dazed and upset. You've been set up, and you're furious at your colleague. You can't understand why she robbed you of this crucial information. You're nervous about going into the meeting unprepared and afraid of the repercussions that her omission will cause you.

Don't Go There

- Don't yell, "How dare you?"
- Don't run to the boss and say, "She didn't tell me."
- Don't rant about her to your best friend at work.

• Don't act out—throwing things or stomping around—to let everyone else know how angry you are.

Go Here

As difficult as this may be, your best move is to take responsibility for the fact that you are not prepared and refrain from blaming your coworker. Immediately go to your boss and say, "I understand that the deadline was changed, and I wasn't here for you to inform me. Unfortunately, I found out too late for me to be prepared. I apologize for the delay, but I can get this to you by the end of the day."

Going Forward

As you hand the project to your boss, make the following request: "To ensure that I know of any changes in the future, please communicate with me directly. If I'm not present, I can always be reached by e-mail." When it comes to your colleague, understand that leaving you uninformed may be her way of competing with you. Don't count on her to have your back.

Coffee Break

Resisting the Temptation to Counterattack

Whenever we have been mistreated by another woman, it's extremely tempting to fight back. Resisting the temptation to counterattack involves becoming aware of how you might want to hurt the woman who's hurting you.

Common counterattacks include ignoring the other woman, rolling your eyes when she speaks, sulking, pouting, bad-mouthing her when she's not in the room, and spreading rumors about her to others.

Resisting the temptation to counterattack requires an awareness of what your revenge tendencies are and a conscious decision not to use them.

She Goes Behind Your Back and Says She Can Do a Better Job

What She Does

It could happen in a number of ways:

- You give a presentation, and your coworker approaches the boss afterwards. She says, "She didn't do a very good job. I could come up with a better presentation."

- You're working on a design for the marketing department, and a colleague tells the director, "If you want fresher ideas, give the assignment to me."

- You're a teacher or trainer, and you call in sick. The woman who substitutes for you goes directly to your supervisor after the class and says, "I'm a more qualified instructor. I'd like to replace her."

How You Feel

Upon learning of your colleague's behavior, you feel totally betrayed. You can't believe she would stab you in the back like that. You are angry and upset that this woman has had the nerve to put you down and try to insert herself into your job.

Don't Go There

- Don't blow a gasket when you first learn about her behavior (either from a peer or from your supervisor).
- Don't start bad-mouthing her to other people.
- Don't shut her out.
- Don't take her words or her behavior personally—she's not better than you.

Go Here

This is a situation in which confrontation is a must. You must go to your colleague in person and say, "I know that you are telling others that you could do a better job than I can. I'm sure you can get your own work without taking mine." Even if she denies that she tried to encroach on your territory, she now knows that you are onto her game.

Going Forward

You now know that this person has no compunction about promoting herself at another person's expense. For her, all is fair in self-promotion at work. Unfortunately, most people who go after other people's jobs believe that the only way to get ahead is at someone else's expense.

Your job is to maintain a high profile professionally and not let her get under your skin. Trust that others are aware of her shameless behavior, and, stick to building on your own accomplishments.

She Gives You and Another Woman the Same Assignment

What She Does

It's Tuesday morning, and your boss proudly hands you a nice juicy project: come up with an online survey for the company's newest line of products. You are really excited because this is right up your alley. You go home and begin working on the survey immediately. You have so many ideas that you can't wait to get started.

The next morning, you walk into the office and run into a colleague who announces that the boss had asked her to create an online survey. "What?" you say. "How can that be? She asked me to do the same thing yesterday!" Shrugging her shoulders, your innocent coworker says, "I don't know what to say. She asked me to work on it yesterday, and I sent it in this morning."

How You Feel

You feel confused, deflated, disappointed, and very angry. Your head is spinning. You feel that you've been duped.

Don't Go There

- Don't go marching into your boss's office and blast her.
- Don't blame your boss for poor judgment or bad decision making.
- Don't make it obvious to your coworkers that you are angry.
- Don't assume that the boss thinks you are incompetent.

Go Here

Go directly to your boss and ask for a few minutes of her time. Let her know that you'd like to understand how you and your colleague were given identical assignments. Find out if she still wants you to work on this project. After you hear her reasoning, you will have to determine whether giving two people the same assignment is her management style.

Perhaps this was a one-time event, and she forgot that she had already assigned the project. If she says that she didn't know whether you would deliver the survey on time, you can request that in the future she give you a chance to prove your ability to meet a deadline.

Going Forward

Your boss may have trouble trusting anyone to deliver. This is her problem—but you will have to live with it. If mistrust is at the root of her behavior, she will probably double-assign projects in the future. One thing you can tell yourself is that her behavior is not a personal statement about you. She does this to everyone. The next time this boss gives you a project, ask around to find out who else received the same assignment. Learn to enjoy the teamwork.

She Says Yes when She Really Means No

What She Does

Your coworker agrees to help you on a special project, pitch in on a deadline-driven proposal, or assist you at a company event. When the project, deadline, or event rolls around, this same individual suddenly fails to show. You are left high and dry and scrambling on your own.

When you ask your coworker what happened, she denies making any promises: "I didn't say that. You must have misunderstood me." Or she may come up with a lame excuse: "My boyfriend broke up with me, and I forgot." Whatever the response, you get the feeling that she takes no responsibility for the trouble she's caused you.

How You Feel

Being left high and dry by a supposedly friendly colleague is very confusing. You feel betrayed, let down, and angry. You can't believe that this person could be so inconsiderate. You also can't understand what happened. "She gave me her word," you think to yourself. "How could she do this to me?" You rehash the series of events that led up to this apparent misunderstanding. To make matters worse, you don't even have time to process your feelings, because you now have to do the work of two.

Don't Go There

- Don't run around and disparage this woman to everyone you know.

- Don't give her the cold shoulder or stop talking to her for weeks at a time.

- Don't confront her and insist that she admit what she failed to do; this kind of person only gets defensive when you do that.

Go Here

First, take some time to recover from your experience. Do whatever you need to do to cool off. You may want to exercise, talk to a friend away from the office, get a massage, or take a long scenic drive. Eventually, you'll need to have a conversation with your colleague, and you'll want to do so when you're in a calm (not heated) emotional state. Once you've cooled off, you can approach her and say, "I'm not sure what happened, but I thought we had an agreement. To avoid this kind of misunderstanding again, I'll send you an e-mail confirming any agreements we make."

This solution may seem too lenient, but if you are to maintain a relationship with the yes/no colleague, you have to avoid accusing her of dropping the ball.

Going Forward

While you may have built a bridge back to working with this individual, it's important that you recognize that she is not on your list of reliable coworkers. Keep the relationship superficial and professional. Try to create situations in which there are witnesses to any agreements—other people who see you both make a commitment. If you feel it necessary to warn others, you can suggest that they too send written confirmations of any tasks that she agrees to do.

Coffee Break

Strike when You've Cooled Off—Not in the Heat of the Moment

Used constructively, anger can serve as your protection. But lashing out in anger or yelling at someone in the heat of the moment puts you in a compromised position. You might say something that you regret, and your angry outburst may seem out of proportion to the offense. Neither of these outcomes will improve your situation.

You'll appear more professional (and be more powerful) if you speak or write to a woman who angers you from a position of calmness and clarity. The next time someone at work says or does something that maddens you, do your best not to react. Instead, take a slow, deep breath and calmly respond with neutral statements like, "Is that so?" "Interesting," "Hmmm," or, "Let me think about that."

Then, take the time to chill: splash your face with cold water, exercise, call a friend, or walk the dog. Do something to cool your system down. Once you relax, you can come up with an appropriate, professional response.

She Says Things That Sound Good but Feel Bad

What She Does

Sometimes you meet a woman who is ostensibly supportive, but who rubs you the wrong way. When you come to work in a new outfit, she may say, "That suit looks great on you. It totally offsets your hips." Or when you finish giving a Power-Point presentation to the entire department, she may assure you, "I really liked it. Don't worry about the people who were nodding off." When you ask for her feedback on a professional article that you'd like to submit, she encourages you, "For really basic writing, it's very good."

How You Feel

While you may smile as she delivers her zingers, you feel as if she's gently punching you in the stomach. You're not sure how to respond. You'd like to believe that she wants the best for you, yet her words don't hit you in a "nice" way.

Don't Go There

- Don't ask her what she means by her comments.
- Don't try to defend yourself.
- Don't tell her off.
- Don't go to your friends and analyze her behavior.

Go Here

Understand that you are dealing with a very covertly competitive woman who needs to let everyone around her know that she's slightly superior. A colleague like this can shake your confidence, so remind yourself that her comments are designed to put you in a weaker position. To the best of your ability, shake them off and move forward.

Going Forward

Find other women who can guide and support you—and who do not have a hidden agenda. You may want to seek a mentor or look for a mature, secure woman who is willing to offer constructive advice and feedback (in a supportive manner) to counteract your competitive coworker's caustic compliments.

JUST BETWEEN US GIRLS

Passively mean girls offer a valuable opportunity for both professional and personal growth. To stop a passively mean girl from practicing her various types of indirect aggression, you must be willing to confront her in a clear, nonemotional manner. The way to straighten things out with this covert colleague is to do exactly what she's incapable of doing—be direct.

You may need to use a coach or a mentor to find the best wording. You may have to practice saying, "Please do not exclude me from future e-mails," or, "I'd appreciate it if you wouldn't tell others that you can do a better job than I can." And you'll need to be prepared for the passively mean girl to deny whatever behavior you accuse her of.

Trust that, with time and experience, you will get better at confronting a passively mean female. And know that learning how to state your case in a calm, confident voice will serve you well in the future. Once you confront this coy coworker, she will rarely have the nerve to continue competing with you in the same way.

CHAPTER 5

Doesn't Mean
to Be **Mean**

There's a certain kind of woman who really doesn't mean to be mean, but whose actions often seem offensive and hurtful to others. These women may be very friendly. They are often kind in spirit, and they appear to be well intentioned. And yet, they are extremely self-absorbed. They literally aren't aware of how their unconscious, inconsiderate behavior affects others.

Have you ever experienced any of the following?

- When your coworker arrives late for a meeting, she's surprised that you're mad because she has kept you waiting (again).

- When her messy desk has made it impossible for you to find an important document, she can't understand why you're so upset.

- Even though her depressed mood immobilizes her, putting your project in jeopardy, she's startled when you suggest that she get help.

Women who "don't mean to be mean" are a study in self-centeredness. Unlike "meanest of the mean," "very mean," and "passively mean" girls, who can really inflict pain and damage on your life, these women don't intend to attack you. Rather, they are so immersed in their own thoughts, feelings, and dramas that they don't consider anyone else's reality. They truly are oblivious.

If you are someone who is extremely concerned about the welfare of others and who goes to great pains to be considerate and caring toward everyone around you, you'll find this type of woman maddening. In fact, you won't believe that she doesn't know better. Her thoughtlessness will seem selfish and unsupportive to you. The key to handling a woman who doesn't mean to be mean, but whose self-centered actions drive you crazy, is twofold:

1. **You must not take her behavior personally.** Whether it's habitual lateness, chronic disorganization, serial illnesses, or some other kind of drama, this individual is not targeting you. She's simply self-absorbed, and you happen to be in her orbit. You can rest assured that she treats everyone the same way. And she's not going to be changing any time soon.

2. **Learn how to set boundaries with this person.** This means that you find ways to limit the negative impact of her "mean" behavior. Instead of waiting for your doesn't-mean-to-be-mean colleague to change, implement systems that protect you professionally. For example, if you work with a colleague who is chronically late, establish time

boundaries for anything you do with her. Tell her that you'll wait 15 minutes for her at any meeting or event, and if she doesn't show, you'll either leave or start without her.

If you're a nice girl, this kind of person will be a challenge for you. You may vacillate between moments of total frustration, feeling sorry for her, and demanding that she change. Don't let your feelings about her behavior get in the way. Stay professional by focusing on managing her behavior.

She Spreads Rumors

What She Does

You're coming into work, and you find yourself riding the elevator with the company receptionist. She leans over and says, "Did you hear the latest?" Your ears perk up, and you say, "No. What?" And she whispers, "The big boss is on his way out. He'll be let go by the end of today."

The next day she has another tidbit to share, "I wouldn't get too comfortable," she says. "I understand we're being absorbed by another company, and they won't be needing most of us." "When is this happening?" you ask. "Soon. They're working out the details."

A week later, this same person approaches you in the ladies' room. "Any news on the merger?" you inquire. "It's not looking good," she whispers. "The buying company doesn't like our financials."

How You Feel

At first, you're excited to be privy to this inside scoop. You're also nervous about the ramifications of each rumor. How will it affect you? What will happen to your department or the company? You feel distracted and unable to focus on work.

Don't Go There

- Don't assume that the rumor is true.
- Don't spread the rumor to anyone else (digitally or otherwise).
- Don't engage in conversations about the rumor until you have more solid information.
- Don't start looking for another job.

Go Here

As difficult as it may be, do your best to mind your own business and get down to work. Until you have confirmation of this information, act as if you don't know it. Even if the story is true, you don't want to be viewed as someone who helps spread rumors at work.

Going Forward

The next time the rumor spreader approaches you, act uninterested. With time, she will get the message that you are interested only in the facts, not in idle gossip that hurts company morale.

Coffee Break

The No Gossip Diet

We challenge every woman reading this book to take our 30-day No Gossip Diet. It may be difficult, but, like anything that's good for you in the long run, it's worth the effort.

Here is how it works:

1. Pick a start date. Mark it on your calendar.

2. Tell your friends. Tell everyone you normally talk with that you're going on a No Gossip Diet for 30 days. See if anyone wants to join you.

3. Keep a daily journal. Beginning on Day 1, write down the number of times you zip your lip, walk away from a conversation, or hold in what you really wanted to say to avoid gossiping.

4. Notice who the gossip girls are. Who in your circle of friends tries to get you to gossip, even though they know you're on a diet?

5. Notice how many of your relationships are built around gossip.

6. See how you feel after 30 gossip-free days. You may decide that gossip no longer fits your lifestyle.

She Just Doesn't Do Her Job, Making You Look Bad

What She Does

You're working on a team project, and your part of the project depends on your coworkers giving you her finished work. It could involve:

The photos needed for the company holiday card

The copy for a website so that you can complete its design

The financial information required to be plugged into an annual report

Time is passing, and you've requested the material that you need from this person several times. With each request, your colleague assures you that she's working on it and that you'll receive it shortly. Your deadline is approaching, and you haven't received anything from her. Your boss is angry with you for not managing the project. "I don't understand why you're not meeting your deliverables," he complains. "Just get the job done."

How You Feel

You feel angry, frustrated, perplexed, and deceived. You can't understand what's holding your colleague up and why she keeps promising results that she cannot deliver. You lose faith and trust in this person, and you wonder what you may have done wrong to create this situation. You also feel stressed out because others are waiting for the finished product.

Don't Go There

- Don't complain about your colleague to the boss.
- Don't take her behavior personally—you did not cause her failure to deliver.
- Don't yell at her for ruining your reputation.

Go Here

Gather the proof—e-mails, notes, and meeting agendas—that your colleague has missed every deadline that she's set, and approach her with these documents. Set up a phone call or an in-person meeting where you let her know that this is the last opportunity for her to rectify the situation with you before you report her to the boss. Say, "I want us both to succeed, so how do we work this out?"

You may then have to walk her through the exact steps she must take to complete her part of the project. Schedule a time when the two of you will meet so that you can monitor her as she completes each of the tasks required. Overseeing this kind of coworker as she works is probably the only way you'll get her to produce what you need from her.

Going Forward

Should you be paired with this woman again, create a system in which she reports to you on a regular basis. Understand that this kind of person lives in a chaotic state. She is easily confused and overwhelmed. You will probably have to lay out and prioritize all the steps involved with her part of any project. She needs to be monitored and managed if you want her to deliver.

She's Chronically Late

What She Does

There's a coworker you really like, but she always keeps you and others waiting. She slides into meetings 30 minutes after they've begun. She convinces management to adjust her work schedule to accommodate a later start time, but she still walks in 15 minutes late. She makes appointments with you, then texts you at the last minute to say that she's running behind. Even at professional events, this woman shows up long after everyone else. While she's quick to apologize and claims to be "working on it," you're tired of her behavior.

How You Feel

Your colleague's chronic lateness irritates and annoys you. You're angry every time she keeps you waiting. You feel let down by her failure to show up. It seems as if she doesn't respect you, your time, or your work.

Don't Go There

- Don't yell at her for keeping you waiting—it won't change anything, and you'll look like the bad guy.
- Don't shut her out when she shows up late.
- Don't buy her a watch so that she can be on time.

Go Here

Start communicating time boundaries to your chronically late colleague. The next time you make an appointment with this woman, let her know that you'll wait 15 minutes from the actual appointment time, and if she's not there, it will be her responsibility to reschedule with you. Then follow through on your end. If she does not appear within 15 minutes, leave the situation.

Going Forward

Understand that this kind of person will not change until she's ready to do so. The best you can do is to protect yourself by continuing to set time boundaries. If you are running a meeting and she's late, start the meeting without her. Tell your tardy colleague that she is responsible for getting the notes about what happened in her absence. If you have to make a presentation with this person, let her know that you'll be prepared to begin the presentation on time—whether she is present or not. Taking care of yourself professionally increases the chances that she will be held accountable for her lateness problem.

She Continually Dumps Her Work on You

What She Does

It can happen in a number of ways. She has a doctor's appointment (again) and begs you to finish her project. She claims personal emergencies that require her attention and pleads, "Can you help me out?" She keeps telling you how smart you are and how much faster you can do the data analysis. While you keep shouldering a good portion of her workload, you never get the sense that her need to pass off assignments will end.

How You Feel

Over time, you feel used and resentful. You wonder if she thinks that you are her maid or servant. You also feel trapped. Since you've agreed to help her out so many times, you're afraid that if you say no, the work just won't get done. You think, "Her unfinished assignments will land on my desk anyway."

Don't Go There

- Don't go to the boss and complain.
- Don't talk to everyone you know about what a drain she is and how sick you are of shouldering her workload.
- Don't throw the work back at her in a rage.
- Don't leave the work undone and passively get her in trouble.

Go Here

The next time she attempts to pass her work on to you, break the cycle. Instead of taking it on, say, "I'm sorry, but I've got too much to do. I can't help you out this time." Then walk away or return to your own work. This sounds simple, but it's often difficult to do. You may fear that your coworker won't like you and will hold a grudge. To build a bridge, you can say, "If you'd like, I'll go with you to our boss and see if we can get the workload in this department redistributed."

Going Forward

Get comfortable with saying no (politely) to this kind of coworker. Women who habitually pass their work on to others will test you continually until they realize that you won't comply. Have faith that she will find another unsuspecting colleague to shoulder her responsibilities. Just say no in the kindest way.

She Is Less Organized than You Are

What She Does

You have a coworker who is very bright, but whose work area is always in chaos. Her desk is covered with papers, paper napkins, and empty coffee cups. She claims to know what is in the piles that surround her, but she can't find a document when you need it. If you give her something to hold, she often misplaces it. You both end up spending hours searching for the materials you need to complete a project.

How You Feel

This kind of colleague is extremely frustrating. You feel exasperated that you have to deal with her chaos. Her disorganized way of operating makes you angry and anxious. You can't trust her to come through for you at work.

Don't Go There

- Don't blow up at her.
- Don't try to reform her by buying her organizing systems.
- Don't rescue her by spending hours trying to reform her behavior.

Go Here

Instead of trying to organize or rescue this person, come up with your own system for holding her accountable. If you have to do a project together, give her a list of the tasks that she must perform, with deadlines attached to each item. Send her reminders of what she's agreed to do before each meeting. Also, keep copies of anything that she produces for you so that you don't have to waste time digging through her piles of files.

Going Forward

Disorganized people do not mean to make your life more difficult. The most challenging thing in this situation is refraining from trying to reform her or correct her behavior. Another challenge is not feeling victimized by her chaos.

Create a backup system for everything you receive from your disorganized colleague. You may not like acting as her workplace nanny, but remember that you're doing this to protect your reputation. Do your best to hold her accountable, and stay focused on the work at hand.

Coffee Break

Reduce Her Abuse by Setting Limits

If you feel continually victimized by someone's behavior, you may have more power than you think. You may not be able to change her behavior, but you can limit the negative impact that her lateness, sloppiness, thoughtlessness, or moodiness has on your work life. The key is to set limits.

Setting limits with a coworker takes practice, and it can be scary at first—especially if you're uncomfortable saying no and afraid of being disliked—but if you want to move forward in your career, it's a vital skill.

How do you set a limit?

Start by identifying the behavior that's driving you crazy. Does she keep asking you to cover for her? Is she always depressed? Does she constantly ask you for help no matter how busy you are?

If you can pinpoint what she's doing, then you can decide what you are no longer willing to do:

> "I'm sick of covering for her. I don't want to do it anymore."

> "I'm tired of always trying to make her feel better when she's depressed."

> "I don't have time to help her. I can barely finish my own assignments."

From there, you can establish and communicate your limit. Some ways of doing this are:

- The next time she asks you to cover for her, you say, "I'm sorry. I'm not going to be able to do it this time."

- When your depressed colleague comes looking for sympathy, you say, "I'm really busy right now. I'll check in with you later."

- If your needy officemate asks for help, you say, "I'd like to, but I'm overloaded myself at this time." Then walk away.

You may fear that setting a limit will get you in trouble. The person on the receiving end may not like hearing you say no, but she will find someone else to do her bidding. Trust us on this one.

She's Always Depressed

What She Does

You may have a coworker who seems sweet, but troubled. As you get to know her, you find out why she seems so sad. She's depressed. She may have health problems, weight problems, financial woes, or family losses. She may be going through a difficult breakup, suffering through a bitter divorce, or worried about her sickly child.

Whatever her issues may be, they're bringing her down. Her face looks glum, her energy is heavy, and there seems to be a dark cloud around her. She may be quick to anger or be on the verge of tears. She's suffering, and just being in her presence can pull you down emotionally. You find yourself trying to prop her up and help her feel better. Her personal issues often interfere with her ability to get work done.

How You Feel

Spending time with this kind of depressed person is draining, exhausting, and sad. On the one hand, you feel sorry for her and all her problems. On the other hand, talking with her is not very uplifting. Listening to her sad stories, consoling her day after day, or just being around her can really bring you down. You may even start to feel trapped.

Don't Go There

- Don't tell her to snap out of it and look at the bright side of things.
- Don't feel obligated to be her unpaid social worker.
- Don't keep handing her phone numbers for therapists and psychiatrists.

Go Here

It's important to realize that depression really can be contagious. To build your immunity, work on creating some emotional distance from this person. The next time you see her, steer the conversation away from personal issues and toward work. Keep redirecting your interactions until you are both focused on whatever work issues you share.

Going Forward

In response to your emotional distancing, this coworker may redouble her efforts to get you back as her unpaid social worker. She may come to you with more sad news or start crying at your desk, trying to elicit your support. She may get angry and say, "You've changed," or, "Are you OK? You seem mad at me."

These pleas for attention may pull on your heartstrings, but resist the temptation to be drawn back in. Instead, say, "I still care about you, but we need to get back to this project."

She Uses Health Problems to Get Attention

What She Does

It starts with a migraine headache that your colleague suddenly develops during a meeting. She tells you that her head is throbbing, and you quickly administer aspirin and usher her to a dark room. A week later, she has a severe allergic reaction to the office's new carpeting. This time, you fetch her Kleenex and offer her your workspace so that she doesn't suffer from the fumes.

Two weeks later, this same coworker hobbles into work on crutches. She broke her foot over the weekend; she sighs, "I don't have very good luck when it comes to my health." Now you are bringing her coffee, ordering her lunch, and going to the printer to pick up her reports. As you help her into her car at the end of the day, you notice that you're spending a lot of time catering to your ailing colleague.

How You Feel

This kind of situation is very confusing. On the one hand, as a caring person, you derive a certain amount of satisfaction from helping your impaired coworker. At the same time, however, you also feel used and manipulated. You are trapped in the role of her caregiver, and you don't know how to escape. You also feel drained, as catering to her needs eats up your time and energy and never seems to let up.

Don't Go There

- Don't go to the boss and call your colleague a hypochondriac.
- Don't believe that you have to be her daytime servant.
- Don't roll your eyes every time she talks about her ailments.

Go Here

The best thing you can do in this situation is to learn how to set limits. You may let your colleague know at the beginning of the day that you have a heavy workload and won't be available to assist her. To soften the blow, you can start the day by helping her in a small way—getting her coffee, bringing her tissues, or listening to her complain about her health. Then say, "OK, I've got to get to work now," and make yourself scarce.

Going Forward

Make it your goal to limit your caretaking role with this person. Find ways to show concern without being enrolled to do her bidding. Understand that her ailments are the only way she knows to get attention and accept the fact that she will always develop new health emergencies.

She's Very Moody

What She Does

Depending on her mood, this person seems to run hot or cold toward you. Some days, you encounter a smiling, friendly colleague. On other days, she's quiet and withdrawn. If you catch her at the wrong time, she may snap when you ask an innocent question. At another moment, she may break into tears and confess her boyfriend problems. Her moods are like weather fronts: they roll in and dominate the office. The bottom line is, you find yourself walking on eggshells around her. You can't tell whether she's your friend or your frenemy.

How You Feel

After a few experiences with this edgy individual, you find yourself being cautious in her presence. You may hesitate to approach her. When she lashes out, you feel stung and upset. You find yourself gauging her mental state. Over time, you simply avoid her.

Don't Go There

- Don't tell her off or call her the Office Downer.
- Don't go complaining to others about her.
- Don't try to kill her with kindness—it won't help her moods.

Go Here

This may be one of those situations where your supervisor or boss can help. Approach him or her and explain that the power of this colleague's mood swings is having an adverse impact on everyone else in the department. You can emphasize your coworker's capabilities, but explain that the situation needs to be addressed by someone in a management position. Ask your boss or supervisor to assist your turbulent coworker. Perhaps she can be taught how to manage her moods and improve her communication style.

Going Forward

Whether or not management is willing to address this situation, the key for you is to learn to detach from your moody colleague's stormy behavior. Try not to absorb her bad moods. In fact, you want to learn how to notice her emotional state (happy, angry, sullen, or sad) without making it your job to manage that mood. Stick to the business at hand, and address your colleague expecting a professional response—whether she can deliver it or not.

You've Helped Her, but She Won't Help You

What She Does

Some workplace friendships start out with a bang and quickly go downhill. This kind of coworker is very friendly at first, and very grateful for your assistance. When you show her how to upload documents, update the database, or solve another business problem, she's very appreciative. She seems to need your help a lot, and you enjoy giving it. A workplace friendship quickly develops. The two of you become quite chummy. You share personal stories, eat meals together, and enjoy each other's company.

At some point, you need a hand. It may be the overhauling of an office system or a huge order that needs to be fulfilled. It's something that your coworker is very adept at, so you ask her for assistance. She seems surprised and annoyed. "I'm really busy," she declares. "Ask me later." A few days later, as you feel more desperate for help, you shoot her an e-mail, send several texts, and leave two voice mails. There's no response. Finally, you catch her smoking a cigarette outside, and you say, "Hey, can you give me a hand?" She rolls her eyes and replies, "I don't have time for that kind of thing. Find someone else to help."

How You Feel

You feel let down and used. You're mad at your coworker, and you're desperate for help. You feel betrayed. Her earlier gestures of interest and kindness seem empty now. The whole situation is extremely unfair.

Don't Go There

- Don't bad-mouth her to your peers.
- Don't go to the boss and report her bad behavior.
- Don't keep trying to make her help you.

Go Here

First, do something to purge your negative feelings about this person. Any kind of physical activity will do. The idea is to cool down your system so that you can approach your colleague from a calm place.

Once you've cooled down, go to her and say, "I really helped you with the expectation that when I needed help, you'd be there for me." She'll do one of several things. She may apologize and give you a hand. She may sigh and reluctantly give you minimal assistance. Or, she may say, "I don't owe you anything. It's your job to figure it out."

Going Forward

At work, reciprocity is not guaranteed. The fact that you are a helpful person is a good quality. In the future, you may want to be more selective, not getting too close and giving too much to someone who's not able to support you in return. You don't have to condemn this person. Just understand who she is—someone with a strong sense of entitlement who does not see the need to return any favors.

Coffee Break

It's Not Fair

It's not fair that you helped a coworker before, and now she won't help you.

It's not fair that you have to run a project with another person who's incompetent.

It's not fair that your boss doesn't appreciate how hard you work.

And it's not fair that an employee whom you manage has a bad attitude.

Now that we've established how unfair it is, what's next? You can congratulate yourself for being right. You've assessed the situation correctly. But that affords limited satisfaction. Your situation won't improve until you do something different. Sorry. It's not fair. But your attitude is what will change your reality.

So accept that the situation you're in isn't fair, and get ready to respond to the difficult people around you differently.

She Excludes You from an Important Professional Decision

What She Does

You think of her as your best friend at work. Then something happens. It may be a promotion, a job change, or some other decision she makes without telling you:

- She interviews for a position at another company, but doesn't say anything until she receives a firm offer.
- She gets promoted within the department, but doesn't inform you until the boss announces it.
- She terminates a fellow employee and keeps it a secret until the person walks out the door.

- She elects to move to another state and doesn't tell you until she's finalized her plans.

Whatever the decision is, your closest workplace friend keeps it to herself. This seems odd to you because the two of you have confided so much private information to each other in the past.

How You Feel

Upon hearing the news, you're initially stunned. That surprise quickly turns to feelings of anger and betrayal. You're hurt that your friend shut you out from such an important life decision.

Don't Go There

- Don't act out your hurt feelings by yelling at her or putting her down.
- Don't ignore her or shut her out.
- Don't lecture her on what a good friend you've been to her, while she's broken your trust.

Go Here

Take a couple of days to soothe your hurt feelings and cool off. Then approach your friend privately and let her know how you feel. Say, "I was hurt and surprised that you didn't tell me about this in advance. I thought we had a close relationship, and I don't understand why you weren't able to confide in me." Then, be open to hearing her explanation.

Going Forward

Some women have an unspoken pact with their girlfriends that they will not keep any secrets from each other—no matter what. While this is a nice idea, it simply isn't realistic in certain work situations. It may take a while for you to recover from this incident. With time, you may see that her behavior was an act of professional discretion rather than a personal betrayal.

She's Overly Controlling

What She Does

Her intentions may be good, but her behavior drives you crazy. Whenever you ask her for something, she needs to know what it's for. She tracks your comings and goings, and she seems to know about every meeting and every project you're involved with. If you have a shared assignment, she needs to make all the decisions. Should you try to add your ideas, she'll tell you why they won't work and explain why her concepts are better. During shared presentations, she dominates the conversation. When a question is asked, she answers for both of you.

How You Feel

Her controlling behavior leaves you feeling trapped. When you are around her, you feel stifled, muffled, and held back. You grow increasingly angry as she continually insists on doing everything her way. You may also feel disrespected and dismissed. You may wonder if you're doing something to trigger her controlling behavior.

Don't Go There

- Don't yell at her to back off and leave you alone.
- Don't roll your eyes, sigh, or otherwise act out in her presence.
- Don't fight her for control.

Go Here

Most controlling coworkers are not intentionally making your life difficult. They overfunction to reduce their own anxiety. Their big underlying fear is that unless they put their imprint on everything, the company won't see their value. In other words, they control because they need to be needed.

Going Forward

The best you can do is twofold: (1) give your colleague constant credit for her ideas, plans, and opinions, and (2) find a way to insert your input (with her permission). You can say something like, "I really appreciate your expertise and knowledge. At the same time, I'd like to participate more in the decision making between us. How can we do that?" You'll probably have to repeat this conversation with your controlling coworker on a regular basis. If you persevere, however, she may be able to let you in.

She Flaunts Her Social Status

What She Does

Always dressed in designer outfits, this woman has a way of assessing other women with one up-and-down glance. The walls of her office are lined with photographs of lavish vacations, spectacular homes, and beautiful children. She casually mentions her favorite four-star restaurants. You learn about her club, her social activities, and her friends who own homes in exclusive neighborhoods.

You notice that she sports a different expensive handbag every month. When she leaves for the day, she drives out of the company lot in a luxury car. You sometimes catch her checking out your attire. It's intimidating to sit with her in a meeting when you know that you bought your outfit off a bargain sale rack.

How You Feel

Her material wealth may be intimidating to you. Sitting in her company, you may feel jealous, angry, resentful, and competitive. You may feel "less than" in her presence. At the same time, you may be tempted to judge her lavish lifestyle and want to put her down. You may assume that since she has so much, she should be generous to you.

Don't Go There

- Don't compare yourself to her.

- Don't criticize her appearance or her behavior with your colleagues.
- Don't feel sorry for yourself because she has all the luck.

Go Here

If you find yourself feeling threatened by a female colleague who flaunts her social status and material wealth, be aware of your judgment and keep it in check. Make a conscious effort to treat her cordially. And refrain from comparing her outer status to your inner worth.

Going Forward

Feeling threatened or intimidated by another woman's social status and material wealth often signals that you may have a desire to prosper. Instead of putting her down, tell yourself, "There's room for two," and get to work pursuing your own form of social and material success.

Coffee Break

The Comparing Game

Women are very skilled at comparing. Two women can compare the prices at different stores, the medical care at different facilities, or the quality of education at different institutions. Ask a woman to recommend her favorite restaurant, health club, or place to get shoes, and she'll quickly give you a heartfelt referral. Why? Because she's shopped and compared; she knows which one she prefers.

This ability to make comparisons works well in many situations, but not all. Problems arise when a woman compares herself to others and either falls short or feels threatened. A woman may feel threatened when another woman has something over her that she feels insecure about: hair, skin, weight, body shape, beauty, male attention, money, marital status, social affiliations, material possessions (homes, cars, boats, jewelry, or clothing), lifestyle, education, leisure activities, professional connections, heritage, children, or family reputation.

If you catch yourself feeling "less than" around another woman at work, check to see if you're caught in the comparing game. If so, remember this slogan: "Compare and despair." Instead of spending time comparing yourself to another woman, focus on becoming your best professional self.

And if you sense that a female colleague is comparing herself to you, zero in on one of her qualities and tell her that you appreciate this aspect of who she is. It may be her forthright behavior, her great sense of humor, her sense of style, or her technological savvy. Noticing and acknowledging the qualities that other women possess can diminish the effects of a negative comparing game.

IN HER OWN WORDS

She's Jealous of Your Looks

It's the morning after the holiday party, and Erin passes by Cynthia on the way to her desk. "You certainly turned heads last night," Cynthia remarks.

"What do you mean?" Erin asks.

"The way the VP of finance drooled over you in that red dress, he's sure to give you a promotion."

Stunned by her colleague's comment, Erin asks, "How would that work?"

"Oh, come on," Cynthia quips. "Promotions come easily to someone with your looks." Erin protests, but Cynthia goes on, "But I work as hard as you do. I just don't play the Pretty card."

With that, Erin walks away feeling misunderstood and put down. She's confused because she thought Cynthia was her friend. Cynthia's sarcastic tone triggers bad memories of past comments made by female colleagues: "You're lucky; you don't have to watch your weight." "Are you auditioning for Vogue?" "With your looks, who needs brains?"

Erin goes home and goes out for a run. While she's jogging, she tries to make sense of her conversation with Cynthia. "I've been here before," she thinks. "Cynthia is judging me based on my looks. I know what not to do. It won't help if I yell at her about how hard I work and how difficult it is to be judged by my appearance. And I shouldn't apologize for my outfit or my behavior at the party—I didn't do anything wrong. But I do want to reduce the tension between us."

As she runs toward her apartment, Erin comes up with a plan. She decides that the best way to handle Cynthia is to ignore her jealousy and befriend her woman to woman. The following week, Erin invites Cynthia out to lunch and shares some of the less perfect aspects of her life. She lets Cynthia know that she lost her father at an early age and struggles with self-doubt. Erin also looks for opportunities to praise Cynthia's performance and to highlight Cynthia's talents in front of their boss.

Going forward, Erin realizes that this issue—other women feeling threatened by her appearance—may come up again at work. She becomes more aware of women making assumptions about her based on her looks. She also focuses on bonding with her female colleagues by sharing the less-than-perfect aspects of her life.

She's Jealous when You Get Engaged or Married

What She Does

You may have a very comfortable relationship with a woman who sits near you at work. You both like watching movies and doing yoga. You discuss vacation plans and compare sales at the local stores. The two of you get along just fine. Then you get engaged. Suddenly, she treats you more like an enemy than a friend:

- She walks behind you on her way back to her desk and hits you on the head with some rolled-up papers. Startled, you ask, "Why'd you do that?" She replies, "At least it wasn't a pair of scissors."

- On the day that your officemates plan to throw a surprise shower for you, she asks, "Are you looking forward to your wedding shower today?" You say, "What wedding shower?" She puts her hand over her mouth and says, with a smirk, "Oops!"

- Any time someone mentions your engagement, she rolls her eyes and says, "Not this again!"

At first, you aren't really sure if you are imagining her hostility. After a few incidents, however, her jealousy and anger become crystal clear.

How You Feel

You naturally feel hurt and confused. You're disappointed and offended by her negative attitude toward your good news. It seems unfair that she would mistreat you for getting engaged. A part of you may feel guilty for the positive attention you receive, which she obviously has trouble witnessing.

Don't Go There

- Don't confront her to ask her why she can't be happy for you.
- Don't hide your engagement ring from her sight.
- Don't try to fix her up with a guy—so that she can get engaged, too.
- Don't describe her to your friends as an angry old maid.

Go Here

It's sad but true that certain women will have a hard time when you reach a life goal that they have yet to attain. You don't need to apologize, but you do need to practice compassion. If you discover that your colleague is jealous of your engagement, do your best to act in a respectful manner. Your success may increase her pain. It may remind her of missed opportunities or failures in the same area. It's not her job to be happy for you, so give her space and keep the wedding talk to a minimum around her.

Going Forward

We'd all prefer to have a supportive environment for our life accomplishments, but that doesn't always happen. To retain some kind of positive relationship with your colleague, you may want to ask her out to lunch or to dinner or invite her to grab a cup of coffee with you. The idea is to rekindle the association you had before the engagement. You may both be able to remember the common ground you share that doesn't involve wedding plans.

She's Jealous of Your Youth

What She Does

Sometimes a colleague may like and appreciate you, yet still feel jealous of the fact that you are younger than she is. Her envy may be expressed in strange ways. If you yawn at a meeting, she may say, "Another late night out with your friends?" If you wear high heels, she'll make a face and say, "Don't come to me when you need foot surgery." When you laugh at a text someone sends you, she quips, "You guys are addicted to your phones."

If you're eager to impress your boss with a new project, she chides, "You should gain more actual experience before you jockey for advancement." When you speak up at a meeting, she rolls her eyes and whispers loudly, "She's so young."

How You Feel

After she delivers one of her demeaning statements, you feel confused and hurt. You don't understand what her problem is. You may be tempted to defend yourself or to tell her to leave you alone. You may find yourself avoiding her.

Don't Go There

- Don't attack back by calling her "grandma" or "old lady."
- Don't defend yourself by saying, "You don't know anything about me."
- Don't make fun of her behind her back.

Go Here

Your best bet with this kind of person is to diffuse her envy. You can try humoring her—if she comments on your high heels, you can say, "I know; these things are killing me. But don't they look cute?" Refrain from commenting on her orthopedic shoes. If humor doesn't work, you can diffuse her comments by putting the focus back on her. Say, "Thanks for your wisdom," or, "Thanks for your concern." If she pulls the "she's so young" card during a meeting, smile and try your best not to take it personally.

Going Forward

It may be hard to imagine, but some people just cannot tolerate anyone who seems to have the upper hand. This older woman's snipes are based on her difficulty in dealing with anyone who is younger than she is. Do not take her behavior personally. You didn't cause it, and you won't be the last one to trigger her envy. Treat her respectfully and try not to take her verbal bullets seriously.

JUST BETWEEN US GIRLS

"Doesn't mean to be mean" girls are a study in arrested development. Think of them as big children—eternally hopeful and eternally self-absorbed. They don't think the normal rules apply to them. A chronically late woman is often surprised at how long her commute takes. A woman who uses her health problems to get attention believes that only she suffers from medical issues. Even the woman who is jealous of your age or who flaunts her social status is under the childish illusion that the world revolves around her.

You really have to accept that doesn't mean to be mean girls are fundamentally different from you and that they are not going to change. You also need to understand that whatever these girls do that seems mean is most likely not intentional. It's merely an expression of their self-absorption.

To deal with any of these colleagues in the long run, you've got to practice setting very strict limits. And you must refuse to be used. Don't wait too long for a colleague to arrive or to deliver, don't assist her too much, don't listen for too long, and don't perform too many of her job responsibilities.

~ CHAPTER 6 ~

Doesn't Know
She's Mean

We are now turning to a different category of women at work. These women differ from the other mean girls because their intentions are good; they are not out to harm anyone. Strong individuals who are ambitious and driven, these women express their opinions in ways that sometimes offend and occasionally infuriate others. They say and do things that they think will improve a situation, but they frequently alienate the women around them.

The last thing on the mind of a woman who doesn't know she is mean is to insult someone or injure another woman. Yet, because of the power of her personality, such a woman tends to say and do things that shock and surprise the women around her. If you're on the receiving end when she critiques your appearance, tells you the correct way to do something, or offers unsolicited relationship advice, you may interpret her words as mean.

If you tell a "doesn't-know-she's-mean" woman that her comments are hurtful, she's often surprised. She may feel misunderstood and wrongly accused. She may also think that the recipient is being too sensitive. She believes that people should "grow up," "get over it," and "move on."

A doesn't-know-she's-mean girl sees herself as a truth teller. Her message is supposed to help you. Whether she's telling you that you don't look good in orange or that you shouldn't hand in that sloppy report, she believes that her actions will make things better. What she doesn't realize is that sometimes her delivery can be harsh and that her colleagues don't always want to hear the truth from her.

The key to staying professional with a doesn't-know-she's-mean coworker is to accept the part of what she says that's useful and leave the rest behind. Even if it stings, doesn't it help you to know when your outfit is less than flattering? Aren't you glad that she pointed out the errors in your report before you handed it in?

If you can consider her feedback from its intended helpful point of view, there may be something of value in it. Comments, opinions, and suggestions made by a doesn't-know-she's-mean girl may hurt initially, but they are not vindictive or devaluing like the words of a truly mean girl.

If her style is too aggressive for you and her words rub you the wrong way, you may not want to be friends with her. Still, you can find a way to work in harmony with this kind of woman. First, you need to understand that much of her behavior stems from a need to control or take charge of any situation. The bossy coworker doesn't mean to belittle you through her micromanaging; she just can't tolerate feeling out of control.

Second, you need to know that she's capable of responding positively to feedback from you. Should she do or say something that really bothers you, you can speak to her about it—often with surprisingly positive results. You may want to begin your communication with, "I know it wasn't your intention, but . . . ," then let her know how her actions affected you. Most doesn't-know-she's-mean women will apologize.

She Bosses You Around

What She Does

There's a woman whose position is equal to yours but who seems determined to act like your boss. She tells you to get the coffee for a meeting; she insists that you photocopy any documents; she tells you when to go lunch. If you're both in a meeting, she'll volunteer your services for the more menial tasks. She tells you when you should take your vacation (based on when she wants to take hers), and she always assumes that she knows the company culture better than you do.

How You Feel

Initially, you're shocked at her presumption of authority. You feel diminished because she's constantly ordering you around. Over time, you grow to resent her. You start to have revenge fantasies. You'd like to see her belittled and put down in the same way that she belittles you and puts you down.

Don't Go There

* Don't complain to your boss about her.

- Don't expect her to change.
- Don't yell at her and tell her she has no right to tell you what to do.

Go Here

Rise above your bossy coworker by sticking to the fact that while she may think she has authority over you, she doesn't. The next time she orders you to photocopy a document that you both need, say, "Sure. I'll ask the receptionist to do it if you don't want to." If she tells you when you're supposed to go to lunch, say, "Actually, that lunch hour isn't going to work today. I need to go at 1:00 p.m. instead."

If she insists that you set up the coffee for a meeting, say, "Sure. I'll do it this time, and you can set it up for the next meeting." You may be afraid that your bossy colleague will get mad at you for asserting yourself. While she may not like your sudden independence, she'll probably back off temporarily.

Going Forward

The big challenge with this kind of person is not to take her bossiness personally. Her compulsion to tell other people what to do comes from a deep need to control. She may continue to order you around, but you don't have to comply. Just continue to neutralize her demands by telling her what you will and will not do. Let her know that you want to work with her but that you don't work for her.

She Constantly Offers Unsolicited Advice

What She Does

She comes off as assertive and sure of her convictions. She sees herself as someone who has the answers for others. She believes that her advice is something of value, that listening to her will further your career. But you experience her advice quite differently.

She says things like, "You should wear that color more often; the other colors wash you out." "Don't forget to speak into the microphone. Last time, I could barely hear you." "I know you don't want to embarrass yourself, so you might want to use spell-check more often."

How You Feel

Her remarks surprise you and catch you off guard. While they could be interpreted as supportive, they feel insulting and mean. Heat may surge through your body, causing your face to flush. You may feel hurt, humiliated, and judged. You may be stunned and lose your footing.

Don't Go There

- Don't get defensive and lash back at her.
- Don't glare at her in stony silence.
- Don't let her thoughtless comments damage your confidence.

Go Here

Take a few deep breaths, try to compose yourself, and say, "Thanks for the feedback." Or you can just say, "Thanks." Then ask yourself whether this person's advice is something that's worth taking into consideration. You can either decide that her opinion is unimportant to you or take the grain of truth and work with it.

Going Forward

Now that you know about this person's proclivity for offering unsolicited and unedited advice, handle with care. Most women who are this opinionated offer uninvited, poorly edited suggestions to everyone. Some of what she says may be of value, but much of it may be about her need to feel important—not about your shortcomings. Consider her behavior an opportunity for you to develop a thicker professional skin.

Coffee Break

Before You Offer Advice

Before you offer advice, make sure that the person on the receiving end is open to hearing it. Sometimes we think we know what someone needs to do or say or even wear at work. We're sure that we're right and that if our colleague or client would just listen to us, a certain problem or situation would immediately improve.

But offering unsolicited advice to someone who's not ready to receive it can create more problems going forward. Before you offer advice, stop and take the recipient's temperature. Say, "I've got a few ideas about how to resolve _____. Let me know when you're ready to hear it."

If you're itching to advise a colleague on a personal matter such as her health, her weight, or her love life, you're better off waiting until she requests your input. If you can't hold it in, say, "I'm having a strong reaction to _____. Can we discuss it?" Or say, "I'm really concerned about _____," and see how the listener responds.

It may be hard to zip your lips. You may feel anxious and frustrated. But learning when and how to offer advice is an important life skill. It takes practice to offer assistance in ways that the recipient can accept.

She Critiques Your Appearance

What She Does

Certain coworkers are generally well intentioned, yet they feel that it is their job to comment on your appearance. These women are usually very visual. They have an instant reaction to whatever they see and low verbal impulse control. Sometimes the critique is positive: "I love that color on you." "You're looking great today." "Wow, you've lost a lot of weight." At other times, they are quick to point out anything they don't like: "Those shoes make your feet look big." "You have a stain on your blouse." "Your lipstick color doesn't go with your outfit." "That skirt looks a little tight on you."

How You Feel

As the words come flowing out of your colleague's mouth, you suddenly feel scrutinized and judged. You quickly seek out the closest mirror to check out the area she's just criticized. You feel embarrassed and put down. Her words seem unkind and insensitive.

Don't Go There

- Don't become defensive.
- Don't tell her to #$!?* off.
- Don't feel the need to explain why you look the way you do.
- Don't counterattack by negatively critiquing her appearance.

Go Here

As difficult as it may be, your best response is to let her comments roll off your back. Realize that you're dealing with someone with poor self-editing capabilities who thinks that her feedback is helping you. If you can, thank your colleague for the observation: "Thanks for letting me know." Then let it go.

Going Forward

One of the annoying things about women who critique other women's appearance is that while the delivery is wrong, the information is often right. After you've cooled off from the encounter, consider whether you value this person's opinion. If so, put her recommendations to use.

IN HER OWN WORDS

Her Jokes Are Hurtful

Jane and Terry are on their way to an in-house software training session. Terry is sharing how nervous she gets when she is trying to learn a new program. Jane lets out a laugh and says, "Yeah. Last training I couldn't believe how difficult it was for you to do the simplest things. Maybe they should start a class called Software for Dummies!"

Terry immediately gets defensive, "Jane, that's mean!"

Jane shrugs it off, "Only kidding."

At the break, Jane spots Terry across the room and yells, "Terry, are you understanding any of this? Want me to help you turn on your computer?" Jane smiles, winks, and turns back to her work.

Terry feels embarrassed and humiliated. Her face turns red, and she wants to run out of the room. She also wants to tell Jane to shut up. Terry doesn't find her funny. Another colleague at the training, Amber, approaches Terry and says, "That wasn't very nice. Come sit next to me, and I'll help you."

After the training, Amber and Terry walk out together to get a cup of coffee. Amber says, "I've had it with Jane. Why don't we make fun of her the way she makes fun of you? Let's make rude comments about her hair and say we're only kidding."

Terry says, "Thanks for the idea, but I don't want to fuel this situation."

"But you can't let her get away with that behavior," Amber protests. "She thinks she's funny, but she's not."

Terry has another idea. She decides to talk to Jane privately. The next day, she asks to meet with Jane for a few minutes. Terry begins the conversation, "I'm sure you didn't mean to be hurtful yesterday, but you were."

Jane looks surprised. "I was just trying to be funny," she says defensively. "Can't you take a joke?"

"I like a good joke as much as the next person," Terry responds, "but not at my expense. When you make fun of my weaknesses, it discounts my strengths. Please leave me out of your jokes."

Jane shrugs her shoulders and says, "OK. But you'll miss me!"

Terry smiles. "I'm willing to take that risk."

Jane shakes Terry's hand and says, "If I can't make fun of you, I guess I'll have to make fun of someone else."

Coffee Break

Appreciating the Power of Words

Women are adept at using words constructively to support one another; they can compliment one another's attire, notice changes in appearance, verbalize qualities in others, lay out and weigh options, and identify and process feelings.

On the other hand, women can also use words as weapons. A woman can use words destructively to criticize people, places, and things; to nitpick; to complain; to spread rumors; to judge and condemn; to manufacture stories that tarnish someone's image; to gossip; and to put others down.

Think of verbal strength as the female equivalent of male physical strength. Appreciate how powerful words are, and learn to use this gift responsibly. It is every woman's challenge to manage her verbal power.

As with any good superpower, women have to decide whether to use words for constructive or destructive purposes.

She Infringes on Your Territory, Does Your Job, and Makes You Look Bad

What She Does

There's a certain kind of colleague who thinks she's helping you out. She swoops in, takes over, performs parts of your job, and then acts surprised when you react negatively.

- You're organizing a breakfast meeting together, and it's your job to arrange for the food. You call the caterer to place an order and find out that your coworker has already taken care of it.

- There's a skill-building conference you've always wanted to attend. When you go to register, she's already taken the department's slot—even though the skills involved aren't part of her job.

- You send your boss the annual budget he requested, only to discover that she has already given him her own version. When you ask her why she did that, she explains, "I knew it was that time of year. I saw you were busy, so I just sent it to him."

How You Feel

Her constant interventions leave you feeling angry, taken over, and blocked. You don't understand why she can't mind her own business and let you do your job. You resent her need to insert herself and take over when you're perfectly capable of performing these tasks. At the same time, you feel confused when she claims that she's just trying to help.

Don't Go There

- Don't freeze her out.
- Don't talk about her behind her back.
- Don't complain to your boss about her obnoxious behavior.

Go Here

This person has a strong need for attention and affirmation. You will need to approach her and say, "I know you're intentions are good. And I'd like to appreciate your help, but every time you do my job without asking, it makes me look less competent." Then make your request: "Please let me do my job, and I promise to ask for help when I need it." Your colleague will probably apologize and back off.

Going Forward

This conversation will probably improve your situation for a while. In time, however, your overeager coworker may relapse. This is because her secret fear is that she won't be valued unless she does everyone's job. For this reason, she may unwittingly perform some of your responsibilities because of her own insecurity. Try not to take her behavior personally. If she steps into your territory again, simply remind her that you need to be able to perform on your own and that you will ask for help if you need it.

She Takes Credit for Your Ideas

What She Does

It can happen in a number of ways:

- You might receive a group e-mail from your boss congratulating your colleague for an idea that originated from you, followed by an e-mail from her accepting the credit.

- You could be in a meeting where another woman proposes a concept that you just shared with her, acting as if it's her brainchild.
- Or you could be out having drinks with your workplace friend and share a brilliant idea, only to see her claim it as hers the next day at work.

How You Feel

Initially, you're probably shocked. You feel angry, used, duped, and betrayed. You can't believe she would do such a thing. Her brash behavior seems disrespectful and insulting.

Don't Go There

- Don't confront her and yell, "How dare you? That was my idea, and you know it! Who do you think you are?"
- Don't freeze her out.
- Don't key her car.

Go Here

While you don't want to release your anger at her, you do need to talk to this person. You may want to cool down for a few minutes before seeking out your credit-stealing coworker. Tell yourself that you do have options. You'll figure out how to get the proper credit and recognition for your ideas.

Next, speak to your colleague in private. When you meet with her, you can say, "You may not have meant to do this, but you took credit for my idea." If she owns up to her mistake, that's great. You can then ask her to correct the misperception. If she denies taking credit for your idea, then you'll have to do your own damage control. You can finish the conversation by saying, "I guess we disagree on this."

Going Forward

It now becomes your responsibility to wage your own public relations campaign. Instead of letting others shine at your expense, you'll want to take special pains to report on and highlight your best ideas to those who count. Remember that you are an idea generator. Even if your coworker takes credit for one brilliant concept that you originated, trust that you'll come up with many more.

The important lesson for you is to distinguish between the trustworthy and the untrustworthy people in your work environment. Learn to hold your ideas, concepts, and plans a little closer until you can figure out who is capable of hearing a great idea without making it hers.

Coffee Break

When to Take a Conversation Offline

Digital communication (texting, tweeting, posting, or blogging) works well most of the time. But when the words exchanged between two women become emotionally charged, it's best to take the conversation offline.

We know how easy it is to send off a quick response, especially when you're eager to clear a communication off your plate. But trouble emerges when that message is misinterpreted.

- Your e-mail becomes an e-missile.

- Your text message reads like a text torpedo.

- Your Facebook post turns into a Face bomb.

- Your innocent tweet starts a Twitter war.

If the topic is delicate, if you need to deliver tough news, or if you know that the recipient might have a strong emotional reaction to your message, do not use e-mail, texting, or Twitter. Instead, speak in person or on the phone.

Whenever there is any room for misinterpretation, face-to-face communication works best.

She Competes with You for the Boss's Attention

What She Does

She's always fawning over the boss—whether it involves admiring the boss's outfit, quoting a statement of his or hers, or remembering a suggestion that the boss made. If the authority figure is a man, she may wear tight clothes, giggle, and flirt. If the authority figure is a woman, she showers her with compliments. You see her coming out of the boss's office laughing. When she returns from vacation, she brings the boss a special gift.

You can tolerate most of her ploys for getting the boss's attention except when you're in a meeting and she dominates the conversation. At every turn, your colleague jumps in to promote her ideas, recite her successes, and continue flattering the boss. You can't get a word in edgewise. By the end of the meeting, you feel like the party wallflower—marginalized and invisible.

How You Feel

After she dominates a meeting with the boss, you feel defeated. You are furious at your colleague's ridiculous, unprofessional conduct. You're also disappointed in your boss's inability to see through her shameless behavior.

Don't Go There

- Don't mimic her behavior to others.
- Don't try to beat her at her own game by replicating her behavior.

Go Here

Any attempts to bring her down will make you look jealous and petty. Instead, we encourage you to focus on finding a way to shine in a manner that is authentic to you. Whether you want to highlight your work performance, attain recognition from customers and clients, or win industry awards, find your way to be seen as a star. In other words, gain attention from the boss for the value that you bring and leave the sweet talk to your colleague.

Going Forward

Competition in the workplace is a part of life. This particular form of competition can be painful to witness because it leaves you (and others) on the sidelines. The sooner you figure out your strengths—getting along with others, excellent communication skills, or technical expertise—the sooner you can capitalize on those strengths to move your career forward.

She Always Has to Be Right

What She Does

There's a type of female colleague who is very invested in having the correct answer to every question. She's usually quite experienced in her field of work, and she's also a hard worker. At meetings, she's always the first to offer a solution to any problem. If you work with her on a project, she insists that her ideas and her line of thinking are the best. If you offer an idea or opinion that differs from hers, she'll dismiss it. Even if you have a slightly different memory of something that you both experienced, she'll insist that her recollection is the right one. It seems like she's always steam-rolling over others, inserting her way of handling things into every situation.

How You Feel

Working with someone like this is stressful, intimidating, and infuriating. You feel as if you're always going to battle with her. Her constant need to be the expert on every issue feels stifling, controlling, and inconsiderate. You become tired of her pushy, self-righteous behavior. You have fantasies of her being transferred to the overseas division of your company.

Don't Go There

- Don't roll your eyes every time she speaks.
- Don't spend time arguing with her—it won't help.
- Don't shut her out.

Go Here

A person who must always be right is operating from a position of insecure arrogance. She needs to defend her position because her self-worth depends on her being right all the time. As difficult as this may sound, your best strategy is to agree with her first so that she can relax her guard and hear what you have to say. In other words, you have to listen to and agree with her before she can listen to you.

Going Forward

It may not seem fair, but to work well with this person, you'll need to keep practicing the art of listening, then agreeing, then inserting your point of view. You can say things like, "Your idea seems right to me. I might add to it," or, "I'd like to build on your plan with this concept." This will never be an equal relationship, but you can develop a positive professional association over time.

She's More Experienced than You Are and Challenges Your Authority

What She Does

It can happen in a variety of ways:

- During a meeting where you're rolling out the new software program for your department, a senior staff member spends the whole time looking at her BlackBerry. When you ask if she has any questions, she says, "I don't understand what you're saying, and I don't see why you need to spend all this money when the existing software is fine."

- Or you're meeting with an older colleague to give her a review, and as you go over each point, she stares in stony silence. At the end of the review, you ask for her response. She says, "It's hard for me to take feedback from someone with so little actual experience."

- Or as you're discussing plans for a client presentation with a coworker, she interrupts you and says, "You're so cute. You remind me of my daughter when she was your age."

How You Feel

On the one hand, you may feel dismissed, cut down, and defenseless. On the other hand, you may feel indignant and furious. Your colleague's words feel disrespectful and unfair.

Don't Go There

- Don't start crying.
- Don't threaten her by saying, "You don't know who you're dealing with."
- Don't freeze her out.
- Don't disparage her to others.

Go Here

It's important to understand that her negative reaction to you is not personal—even if it feels that way. She is probably feeling uncomfortable and diminished by the role reversal of answering to a younger person.

Instead of fueling that potential interpersonal fire, you want to neutralize it by letting her know that you understand her feelings and would like to build mutual respect. You can respond to her put-downs with, "I can understand how you feel, but I'd like the chance to disprove your assumptions about me." If that statement seems too strong, try saying, "I'm sorry you feel that way. I'd like to find a respectful way for us to work together."

Going Forward

Be willing to put in the time and effort to break the power struggle between you and this more experienced worker. Look for ways to honor and appreciate what she brings to the job, and she will gradually acknowledge your expertise as well. By giving her the recognition and respect that she needs, you should eventually get her respect in return.

JUST BETWEEN US GIRLS

Doesn't-know-she's-mean girls are naturally aggressive and assertive. As a group, they are well intentioned, not mean-spirited. The good news is that this kind of colleague is capable of receiving the same kind of straightforward feedback that she dishes out. If you don't like what she does or if you feel offended by what she says, let her know it.

For those of you who are very sensitive and careful not to offend, it may be a challenge to inform a doesn't-know-she's-mean girl when she steps on your toes. Start your message with, "I know it wasn't your intention but," then let her know that her comments weren't helpful or that she did something that upset you.

See this as an opportunity to provide your righteous colleague with valuable feedback. Then express what you'd like from her going forward. Use her as a catalyst to be more assertive yourself.

CHAPTER 7

She Brings
Out Your <u>Mean</u>

Y ou may not want to hear this, but we find that almost every woman has someone in her life who brings out her meaner side. It may be the woman who talks incessantly while you're trying to work, or the woman who asks so many questions that you can't concentrate, or the drama queen who's always in a crisis of some kind. No matter what the issue is, this woman's behavior is so maddening that it elicits an unkind response from even the nicest girl.

Women who bring out your mean are often surprised by the strong negative reactions that erupt around them. They don't attribute your irritation to something they have done. The coworker who asks so many questions that you snap at her might say, "Boy, you must need a vacation." She has no idea that it was her battery of questions that provoked your hostile response.

Most women who bring out your mean are needy in the extreme. Their actions stem from a need for attention, approval, acknowledgment, or acceptance. They may feel insecure about their looks, their age, their education, or their standing in the company. That insecurity causes them to behave in ways that strike you as obnoxious, invasive, or inappropriate.

To find out whether you work with a woman who brings out your mean, ask yourself the following questions:

- Is there someone at work who causes you to behave in ways you aren't proud of?
- Are you short-tempered around this person?
- Do you interrupt her or cut her off when she's speaking?
- Do you avoid her when you see her walking down the hall?
- Have you ever made fun of her or imitated her with your friends?
- Do you feel sorry for her, yet guilty that you don't like her very much?
- Are you excited when she's out sick or on vacation?

It may be difficult for you to admit that a perfectly nice woman provokes hostile feelings in you. You think of yourself as a friendly, caring person. After you cut her off while she's talking or make fun of her to a coworker, you may find yourself justifying your unkind behavior. "I can't help it," you say. "She just drives me crazy."

The most important quality needed to improve any situation that brings out your mean is a willingness to be honest with yourself. Admit that you are resorting to some form of cruel conduct. Once you own up to your side of the equation, you can implement a more effective strategy for the relationship.

Women who bring out your mean usually engage in forms of behavior that you find abhorrent. Whether it's endless self-promotion, a constant need for attention, or outright rude behavior to everyone around her, these women act in ways that go against your grain. Even the woman who asks too many questions or the nonstop talker strikes you as totally inconsiderate because she sucks your time and drains your energy. *You* would never do these things.

We invite you to think about who in your work life may bring out your meaner side. Then see how the tactics we suggest in these scenarios can be applied to improve your situation.

She Thinks She's Better and Smarter than She Really Is

What She Does

You're at a brainstorming meeting, and all the members of the team are working really hard to come up with great ideas. After 30 minutes of discussion, one woman pipes up, "So what I think we should do is . . . ." She then rehashes everyone else's ideas as if they were hers. This is not the first time your colleague has done this. She also says things like, "If I wasn't here, I don't know where this department would be."

This woman is the first person to introduce herself to any VIP who visits the company. She believes that she is the spokesperson, the self-appointed leader of your group. What bothers you most is the fact that while this woman thinks she's top dog, her actual work is below par.

How You Feel

Every time this woman opens her mouth, you feel frustrated and annoyed. Her grandiosity makes you angry, and you're disgusted by her self-aggrandizing behavior. You also feel manipulated by her.

Don't Go There

- Don't roll your eyes every time she speaks up at a meeting.
- Don't check out whenever she begins to say something.
- Don't gossip about her to your colleagues.

Go Here

You may be surprised at what we're going to suggest here. The truth is, there's very little you can do to prevent this person from behaving the way she does. Her need for attention and acknowledgment will continue to drive her to behave this way. Any attempts to "bring her down" or "straighten her out" will come across as jealousy or pettiness on your part. Consider what you can learn from her self-promotional ways. Ask yourself, "How could I become better at advertising some of my successes?"

Going Forward

Use your bragging colleague as a motivator to champion your own career. Instead of focusing on her as the problem, make a commitment to increase your visibility at work. Speak up more at meetings, send out e-mails announcing the successful completion of your assignments, and insert yourself into more high-profile projects. Your self-important coworker will continue her campaign. Your challenge is to keep the focus on you.

She's a Nonstop Talker

What She Does

You always know where this person is in the office because you can hear her chipper voice. She's got lots of energy and plenty to say. It seems as if she has no filter. She tells you what she had for dinner, what she watched on television last night, whom she ran into at the supermarket, and what her morning routine consisted of. She's a nonstop talker, likable but totally draining.

How You Feel

When you see her coming toward you, you look for a place to hide. You feel a sense of dread at the thought of being held captive by her chattering. You feel impatient, restless, and on edge. You just want to say, "Shut up. Shut up! Will you just shut up!!??" Instead, you stand and pretend to listen to her while your mind charts an escape route.

Don't Go There

- Don't listen to her but complain to others.
- Don't make fun of her when she's not around.
- Don't patronize her by pretending to listen as you stew inside.
- Don't try to avoid her.

Go Here

Let your chatty coworker know that you care about her but that you don't have time to listen. The next time she approaches you, say, "I'd love to catch up with you later. Right now, I just need an answer to my question." Other options include letting her know that you have exactly two minutes and then cutting the conversation short.

Going Forward

Talkers are usually unaware of their effect on others. You may fear that she will be offended if you consistently cut the conversation short, but that rarely happens. Most incessant talkers respond to interruptions by saying, "Oh, OK." They are accustomed to being censored, shushed, and edited by many of the people around them.

Over time, your chatty coworker will learn that you are someone who has little time for talking. She will go to others for that. At the same time, you will always have to manage her talkative nature by setting time limits and sometimes interrupting the story to get what you need (which might include peace and quiet).

She Asks Too Many Questions

What She Does

Whenever you begin to focus on a project, there's one woman in the office who finds you and interrupts you. She's got a bunch of questions. She always has questions. She seems endlessly curious and anxious to please. "How should I prepare for the meeting?" "How do you think I should dress?" "Will there be refreshments served?" "How long does it usually last?" "Should I bring copies of my report for everyone, or should I e-mail it ahead of time?" "What do you think the boss will be discussing at this meeting?" "How do you think I should present my ideas?" "What are you going to talk about at the meeting?" "Will you be taking notes?" And on it goes.

How You Feel

Spending time with this person feels very overwhelming. You appreciate her curiosity, but her barrage of questions is just too much. You want to snap at her. You find yourself giving shorter and shorter responses to her queries.

When she finally walks away, you feel angry and exhausted. You may even feel guilty for resenting her neediness.

Don't Go There

- Don't snap at her, "Stop bothering me!"
- Don't put your hand up in her face and say, "Talk to the hand."
- Don't hide in the ladies' room when you see her coming.
- Don't fake being on the phone with someone as she approaches.

Go Here

Understand that this person is operating from a high anxiety level. Her questions come from a need to please, as well as a desire to be supported. Your best approach is to calmly tell her how much time you have to respond to her immediate questions. You may say, "I have only two minutes; what do you need?" If you don't have time to talk, say, "I'd like to help you, but I can't talk right now. Maybe we can chat in a couple of hours." Your questioning colleague may look disappointed for a moment, but she'll quickly back off.

Going Forward

You can soothe and encourage this overly curious coworker by assuring her that she already has many of the answers she seeks. When she comes with a question, try giving it back to her. You can say, "I don't know; what do you think?" or, "I bet you can figure this out," or, "Your guess is as good as mine," or, "Trust your instincts on this one."

Coffee Break

Accepting What We Don't Like

One concept that is very hard to comprehend, but very powerful when it is practiced, is acceptance. Most people mistake acceptance for something else; they think that accepting a person or thing is the same as approving of it. "I'm not going to accept my supervisor's moodiness. That would be condoning her behavior." Wrong. Acceptance is looking at what is and saying, "This is my reality."

You can accept the fact that your supervisor is moody, even though you don't like it. You can accept the fact that your lazy coworker always finds reasons to dump her work on your desk, but you don't have to complete her assignments. You can accept the fact that you don't like a certain customer without having to forfeit the business.

The simple act of stating what is and accepting it as your current reality breathes some air into the problem, makes it a little less dense, and acknowledges your reality.

When something or someone bugs you today, try accepting it. Just say, "I accept the fact that I'm caught in a traffic jam," or, "I accept the fact that my computer is down," or, "I accept the fact that Joyce talks incessantly." Write down the facts about the people or things you don't like and practice accepting them. You'll be amazed at the results.

She Talks to Her Friends and Family All Day Instead of Doing Her Job

What She Does

You're sitting at your desk, and the woman sitting next to you is once again having an animated phone conversation with her best friend. "Oh my God! You're kidding me! She did not!" You notice that this woman spends an incredible amount of time either texting, chatting, or making personal calls. It drives you crazy hearing her chirp about how busy she is when all you notice is the number of hours she wastes interacting with her friends and family.

How You Feel

You probably want to wring her neck and smash her phone. It feels totally unfair that she can get away with such unprofessional and unproductive behavior. Her voice distracts you, and you find yourself steaming mad.

Don't Go There

- Don't mimic her behavior to all your colleagues.
- Don't confront her—even though it's very tempting.
- Don't grab her phone and throw it across the office.

Go Here

Trust that this woman's work product is suffering. It's only a matter of time before her unprofessional behavior will have consequences. If a superior asks you what this coworker is doing all day, refer that person to her work output. That should speak volumes. In the meantime, get a set of headphones or earplugs to drown out your chatty colleague's personal conversations. This will allow you to do your job in a relatively peaceful and quiet setting.

Going Forward

Remember that it's not your job to render justice in the office. Hopefully, your workplace rewards and punishes employees based on what they produce. This is one of those situations where your colleague's lack of productivity should become apparent. If her poor performance does not catch anyone's attention, you may have to endure this chatty girl until you can arrange to be seated elsewhere. Focus on maintaining a professional demeanor and working around her.

She's Rude to You

What She Does

There's a woman in the office who seems to be lacking some basic social skills. She never responds to your daily greeting of, "Good morning." She never says, "Goodbye," when she leaves. If she needs something from you, she starts her request with, "Get me . . . ." The words please, thank you, excuse me, and I'm sorry are limited to special occasions.

If you ask her how her weekend was, she says, "OK," but she never asks about yours. She doesn't clean her dirty dishes. She's not concerned when the garbage at her desk overflows. When she parks her car in the crowded company lot, she often takes up two spots.

How You Feel

Dealing with this woman is an exercise in frustration. You find her behavior disrespectful and annoying. At the same time, you feel hurt that she doesn't appreciate any of your kind gestures. When you're looking for a parking spot and see that she's taken two, you get mad. "Who does she think she is?!" you say to yourself.

Don't Go There

- Don't retaliate by shutting her out.
- Don't "teach her" manners by shouting, "Please!" when she starts to order you to get her something.
- Don't whisper, "So rude!" under your breath when you pass by her.

Go Here

You probably aren't ever going to be friends with this person, but you also don't have to take her behavior to heart. Her rude attitude is not a personal statement to you. She just doesn't see the need for niceties. With all of the things that could adversely affect your experience at work, you should not give this woman the power to ruin your day.

Going Forward

It's not your job to act as the manners police for your office. Everyone sees your colleague's behavior. Her rudeness will probably limit her career options. The only person who is in a position to correct this individual's conduct is her boss—who is probably perfectly well aware of what she does. Practice letting go of your resentment toward this woman. Focus on being professional.

She's a Drama Queen

What She Does

It could involve her boyfriend, her health, her car, her apartment, her workload, or her most recent client conversation. Whatever the issue, there's a big problem. She sighs; she cries; she stomps around. She's loud and very expressive. At one time, you thought she was sensitive and a victim of circumstances. Now, you realize that she brings the drama on herself. Every day she comes to you with the latest installment: "I almost died driving to work today. I got cut off by this reckless driver—who looked just like my ex-husband!" Her dramas drain your energy and waste your time.

How You Feel

Initially, you may feel intrigued and sympathetic. You may be flattered that this woman shares so many stories with you about her exciting life. Over time, however, you feel used and abused. You're drained from listening to the ongoing soap opera that is her life. And you can't stand the one-way nature of your relationship. You fear that her dramas will get in the way of your productivity. You dread sharing projects with her because her work life is full of chaos. She is always preoccupied with her latest personal crisis.

Don't Go There

- Don't try to solve her problems.
- Don't fuel the drama by getting caught up in her stories.

- Don't get involved as her accomplice—drama queens will try to persuade you to go with them to the police, lend them money, or protect them in some way.
- Don't yell at her or tell her to "cut out the drama."

Go Here

As tempting as it is to engage with this colorful person, your best policy when dealing with a drama queen is to find ways to say no. When she comes to tell you her latest tale, listen for a few minutes, and then politely tell her that you have to get back to work. Don't ask for more details, don't offer solutions, and don't get involved. If she asks you to cover for her or help her in some way, try saying, "I wish I could, but I can't this time." If she asks for your advice, say, "I know you can figure this out." It won't be easy, but stick to your guns.

Going Forward

This person is incapable of living without crises. Many drama queens do not perform well on the job, which may lead to their termination. While we do not suggest that you wait for your coworker to get fired, we do recommend that you keep a healthy distance from her. If you have to work with her on a project, you need to know that she is likely to fall short on her commitments, and be prepared to compensate for her. This approach may not be fair, but it is savvy.

She Always Favors the Newest Hire

What She Does

Some women get inordinately excited when anyone new enters the workplace. It may be a new employee, a new boss, a new vendor, or a new client. What's obvious to you is the way your coworker or boss endows the newest hire with wonderful qualities. A woman who favors the newest hire listens intently to everything the new arrival says, acts impressed by his or her credentials, and compliments whatever he or she does.

While your colleague or boss is working hard at winning the new hire's favor, she is also devaluing those who came before this individual. That includes you. Suddenly your colleague or boss may seem uninterested in your ideas, dismissive of your input, and impatient with your requests. Your ranking changes from first class to third or fourth class in her eyes.

How You Feel

You feel dismissed and discarded. Your heart sinks when you realize that you're no longer part of the inner circle. You wonder what you did wrong and why you are no longer valued. You may also resent being replaced by a new favorite.

Don't Go There

- Don't put the new person down or try to make him or her look bad in front of others.
- Don't double your efforts to reinstate yourself with the colleague or boss who plays favorites.

- Don't obsess about what you may have done wrong to fall out of favor.

Go Here

There's very little you actually need to do to remedy this situation. Most people who favor the newest arrival will be loyal to that individual for only a limited period of time. The biggest challenge in this kind of situation is not taking your colleague or boss's behavior personally. You want to be civil and courteous to the new hire, knowing that he or she will be in your shoes (one of the outs) shortly—as soon as the next new person arrives. Keep doing your job, conduct yourself in a professional manner, and wait for this workplace crush to pass.

Going Forward

Understand that women who favor new arrivals are usually enamored with the early phase (aka the honeymoon phase) of any business relationship. With time, you will see this colleague or boss repeatedly putting new hires up on a pedestal, only to bring them down later. Generally speaking, honeymoon phases last between three and six months.

As your favoring colleague or boss finds flaws in the new person, she will take that person out of the spotlight. This situation requires patience and professionalism. Get accustomed to the cycle, and stick to doing your job.

IN HER OWN WORDS

She Gets Promoted Because She Sleeps with the Boss

It's Monday morning, and Kelly finds out that her colleague Gabriella has just been promoted. This sudden change in her coworker's status seems strange and even creepy to Kelly. At the same time, it sheds a new light on the events of the past six months.

A few months ago, on her way home from work, Kelly spotted a top executive and Gabriella through the window of a posh restaurant; they were holding hands and kissing. Next, Kelly caught Gabriella adjusting her clothes as she returned from that same executive's office. Kelly also noticed that this executive insisted on bringing Gabriella with him on business trips—which seemed odd because Gabriella's performance at work was lackluster.

With the news of Gabriella's promotion, Kelly feels outraged. "I didn't think that women slept their way to the top anymore," she complains. Kelly views Gabriella's behavior as degrading and pathetic. As for the executive, she's lost all respect for him. "I pity his poor wife." Kelly wonders whether promotions based on merit exist at her company.

At that moment, Kelly's cell phone rings. It's her mother. "I definitely want to talk to you," Kelly whispers, "but I need to go somewhere private."

She runs down to her car in the company parking lot and gets her mother back on the phone. After she's described the entire sordid situation, her mother says, "This is a tough situation to weather, honey. You'll probably have trouble respecting this woman, and reporting to her may feel like a joke."

"It is a joke!" Kelly pipes in.

"But don't gossip about her, and don't go to HR complaining about her undeserved promotion," Kelly's mother warns. "I suggest you maintain a professional veneer. Even if you don't like how she got promoted, you're not going to improve your career by attacking her."

"I can be civil to her now, but what does this say about the company?"

"Well," her mother considers, "you'll have to make a decision for yourself in the long run. You may want to look around for career opportunities in other departments or different companies where the ethical practices are less offensive to you."

Kelly's mother signs off with this message, "I suspect that Gabriella's promotion is going to take her only so far. You are building a career based on your actual skills and merit. In the long run, you will have a more sustainable career, so don't waste too much time fretting over this short-term situation."

She Wants to Gossip with You About Others

What She Does

You're new on the job and eager to make friends. When one of your female colleagues asks you out to lunch, you immediately say yes. As you're walking out the door with her, she says, "Have you met our receptionist? She's getting divorced and has three kids with three different men." You say, "Oh."

By the time you order your sandwich, you know who's married, who's divorced, and who's having an affair with the mail clerk. Your coworker drops another bombshell as you finish lunch: "Did you know that the woman you replaced had to be dragged to rehab? I hope you don't find any of her empty bottles in your desk drawer." That's when you realize that this chummy colleague is exceptionally interested in discussing other people's private business.

How You Feel

Discussions with this kind of person may be exciting, intriguing, and a bit shocking. You'll feel like you're getting too much information too soon. At the same time, you may be tempted to encourage her storytelling by asking about your other workmates. As you're drawn into this person's confidence, you may also share intimate details about your own life—which she will receive with delight.

Don't Go There

- Don't go running to her with juicy pieces of gossip.
- Don't confide your innermost thoughts, feelings, or personal details to her.
- Don't assume that she will keep what you say confidential.
- Don't try to correct her behavior.

Go Here

You may enjoy being privy to the private lives of your coworkers through this individual, but she is dangerous. Treat her in a friendly, professional manner, but do your best not to get enrolled as one of her "gossip girls." Do not add to her rumor pot, and do not confide your private information to her. Keep a polite distance.

Going Forward

Understand that exchanging information with the office gossip is a tempting but treacherous pastime. Your professional image will be tarnished if you become associated with her rumor mill. Take pains to refrain from discussing your personal life or anyone else's with this person, and she'll eventually learn that you do not participate in gossip.

Coffee Break

Why Gossip Is So Delicious

Gossip is the ultimate equalizer. It's a sure way to cut someone down to size. If there's anyone whom you feel jealous of, competitive toward, angry at, or betrayed by, a juicy piece of gossip that erodes that person's reputation can be music to your ears:

- Who doesn't want to hear that the mean, controlling boss who made your life miserable got fired herself?

- Why wouldn't you want to tell your girlfriend that
  your condescending female coworker got drunk at
  a client dinner?

Gossip can be entertaining, funny, and a tension
breaker. Many women use gossip to achieve a false sense
of intimacy. A scandalous piece of gossip takes the focus
off the individuals who are interacting and places it on
someone else. Two women gossiping about another person will both come out ostensibly closer. By sharing a
secret about someone else's misfortune, they can feel better about themselves whether justified or not.

JUST BETWEEN US GIRLS

Women who bring out your meaner side provide ongoing lessons in patience and forgiveness. You have to be
patient with their neediness and forgive yourself every
time you slip into mean behavior.

What you must understand is that you will never
be able to give your needy colleague enough attention,
reassurance, clarity, understanding, or support. You cannot fill her void. Whatever you do and no matter how
much you try to help her, it will never be enough. If
you can accept this fact, then you'll be less likely to get

caught in the endless cycle of trying to give her enough attention so that she'll leave you alone.

You can quell your own frustration and irritation by approaching this kind of workplace woman in a cool, calm, professional manner. Do not get too friendly, and put very clear limits on the amount of time you spend interacting with her.

CHAPTER 8

Group
Mean

Women are designed to connect and form communities. Throughout history, they've come together to bond, assist one another, share experiences, and provide support. A group of women that is dedicated to a positive cause can accomplish amazing things. Look at MADD:

In 1980, Candy Lightner, a mother who'd just lost her 13-year-old daughter, pledged to do something about the outrage of drunk driving. Her decision quickly inspired a handful of grieving, determined mothers to join the fight. Though they were united in the cause, they had no office, no money, and no clout. In fact, all they had was sorrow, resolve, and a picture of a pretty 13-year-old girl killed by a drunk driver. They were, as their name suggests, MADD (Mothers Against Drunk Driving).

As their fledgling organization grew, it stood toe to toe against politicians who knew the stats but did not act. It took on a powerful industry that put profit over safety. And MADD proved time and again that it would not be bullied or derailed. In fact, MADD blazed a trail that other organizations have since followed.

Among MADD's accomplishments:

- A mountain of traffic safety and victims' rights legislation
- A drop in annual alcohol-related traffic violations from 30,000 in 1980 to fewer than 17,000 today
- An increase in the legal drinking age from 18 to 21 years of age

This is just one example of the powerful positive impact that a group of women working together can have. However, the flip side of women who pursue positive goals together is the mean girl workplace clique—a group of women that targets and bullies one victim at a time.

Most cliques have a leader. The leader of this negative group is the alpha mean girl. She's tough and authoritative. She's been working there for a while, and she knows how to work the system. She also views all new arrivals as potential threats.

Other members of the mean clique are her followers. You see them trying to win her approval by laughing at her jokes, agreeing with her opinions, and going along with her pranks—usually aimed at unsuspecting female coworkers.

When you enter this kind of hostile work environment, it becomes clear that dealing with this group is a double-edged sword. Either these women like you and want you to join them in cruel activities, or they dislike you and make your work life miserable. Many of the women we interviewed simply could not tolerate being the target of a mean girl clique, and they eventually quit.

Here's an important point: it may be possible to find nice girls within a mean girl clique. Some women join a group of mean girls only because they fear the repercussions of standing outside of the clique. They don't want to be targeted, and they aren't strong enough to stand up against the alpha mean girl's directives.

Here's another important point: most mean girl cliques emerge in companies in which institutional leadership is not strong. Their existence indicates that the company's management is either weak or absent. Lacking a recognized authority to temper their behavior, a group of mean girls can tease, taunt, and otherwise torment another woman without ramifications.

When you're confronted with a mean girl group at work, your best bet is to stay neutral. This is much easier to say than to do. Staying neutral means being courteous without agreeing or disagreeing with their antics. The less you react to what they say or do, the less attractive you will be to this clique as either a target or a recruit. In the long run, you have a decision to make about this job, though: do you want to work in an environment that allows packs of mean girls to rule?

A Workplace Clique Excludes You

What They Do

You've recently joined a firm, and you really like your new job. The company has five onsite staff members (all women) and five other employees who work remotely. The four women who work with you at the office go out to lunch together a few times a week. For some reason, they never invite you to join them. They spend a good deal of time discussing where to go for lunch without any concern for your feelings. After lunch, they return to the office laughing and joking with one another. Their connection also seems to extend beyond office hours—to evenings and weekends.

How You Feel

Regardless of whether or not you like your colleagues, being left out of a workplace clique feels lousy. You may feel lonely, unpopular, rejected, or invisible. You probably feel dismissed and insecure. You wonder why they don't invite you. Have you said or done something to alienate them?

Don't Go There

- Don't believe that their rude behavior says something negative about you.
- Don't tell them off.
- Don't pout, hoping that they will pity you.

Go Here

Create your own lunch dates; this will automatically make you feel better about yourself. Make plans to meet your own friends and professional connections for lunch. Reach out to professional associates with whom you can network. Over time, as you develop relationships with your coworkers, they may reach out to you. At that time, you can choose whether to accept or not.

Going Forward

As new women employees enter the company, be sure to treat them the way you wish you'd been treated. Take each new staff member out for lunch. Make her feel welcome. You can set a new standard for others to follow.

A Workplace Clique Gossips About Someone and Wants You to Join In

What They Do

There is often a group of women at work who consider themselves to be "the insiders." They've been working at the company for a while. They've seen people come, and they've seen people go. They like to congregate and gossip. Their topic of conversation is usually a negative critique about someone.

You walk into the company dining area to eat your lunch, and you come across the insiders sitting around a table talking about the new temporary receptionist. "Did you see what she was wearing this morning?" "Does she have only one pair of pants?" "She can't remember anyone's name or extension." "I heard her call Artie 'Archie,' and he was livid." "I wonder if she even knows our company's name."

You're thinking, "She may not be very bright, but this seems petty." As you sit down at the table, they glance over at you. One of the insiders approaches you and asks, "What do you think of the new receptionist?"

How You Feel

You feel trapped and put on the spot. You know the insiders want you to agree with their assessment. You may not be crazy about the receptionist, but you're hesitant to add fuel to their gossip fest. Part of you knows that joining the conversation would help your standing in their eyes. Another part of you doesn't want to participate in such mean behavior. And you suspect that defending the receptionist would not be acceptable to the insiders clique.

Don't Go There

- Don't add your negative impressions to their conversation.
- Don't run out of the room in fear.
- Don't go to the receptionist and report, "They're talking about you in the company dining room."

Go Here

If you feel that you must say something, try this: "Let me think about it," or, "I have little interaction with her, so I don't really know," or, "That's interesting. I'm not sure." Then go back to eating your lunch or focus on performing whatever task you were engaged in before the insiders tried to enroll you.

Going Forward

The insiders clique is not a group you want to be a part of. Generally speaking, these cliques have little professional power and do not hold the respect of anyone who could further your career. Stick to your job and avoid getting roped into any more of their gossip sessions.

Two or More Women Whisper when You Walk By

What They Do

You've just come out of a weekly meeting with your department, and you walk by two colleagues who usually aren't that friendly toward you. You notice these two women staring at you as if they're judging you. As you walk toward them, they lean toward each other and start whispering. You try to ignore their high school behavior, but your gut says, "They're talking about me, and it's not flattering."

How You Feel

You feel embarrassed, humiliated, and small. You flush with shame and burn with anger. You are extremely uncomfortable in your own skin. You don't know what you did wrong, but you know it feels horrible.

Don't Go There

- Don't approach these women and demand, "Are you talking about me?"
- Don't retaliate by whispering about them when the opportunity arises.
- Don't freeze them out at meetings and business functions.

Go Here

Totally let it go. Remember that you don't really know what they said. Also, remember that even if they were gossiping about you, it does not matter. Women who put other women down are doing it to feel better about themselves. Take the high road and proceed as if the incident never happened. Conduct yourself in a professional manner with these women.

Going Forward

If you need to get this incident off of your chest, confide in someone outside of your professional life—a wise friend who can help you laugh it off. At work, keep a professional distance from your whispering colleagues, and focus on doing your job.

IN HER OWN WORDS

A Workplace Clique Harasses You

Patty sits across the table from her sister, Meg, at a local pub, blinking back tears. She stares into her glass of white wine and says, "I don't know what I could possibly have done to make them hate me so much."

Meg pulls out a tissue from her bag and offers her thoughts about the situation: "Sometimes when there are a lot of women in an office, cliques form, and they can be cruel."

"I know," Patty sniffles. "But why me? I'm a nice person. I just want to do my job."

Patty proceeds to tell her sister how she feels. "I'm so stressed I don't want to go to work anymore. I walk in feeling self-conscious and sick to my stomach."

"Why don't you transfer to another department or look for another job?" Meg suggests.

"I know I should, but I've lost confidence in my abilities," Patty explains.

She then tells Meg the different ways in which the mean girl clique has been harassing her. "They snicker when I walk in, as if they're sharing a private joke about me. They tell me to deliver a report to the wrong partner, making me look stupid. I've caught them I.M.ing about me—ridiculing my clothes, my hair, and the way I walk. One of them calls me Pouty instead of Patty. I hate working there."

"Have you ever told them off?" Meg asks.

"Yes. I yelled at them once, and they denied everything." Patty continues. "They called me 'paranoid.'"

"Have you gone to your boss and reported their behavior?" Meg inquires.

"Yes. My boss told me that they are stellar employees and I need to work it out with them."

"How about HR?"

With that, Patty sighs. "I went to human resources, and the representative advised me to try to resolve my differences with these women because they are high performers for the firm."

"OK," Meg says. "Here's what you need to do." The two sisters then lay out a plan. First, they update Patty's résumé. Next, they launch a job search.

"Investigating opportunities outside of the firm will

help you feel like you've got options," Meg explains. "You need to go on interviews so that you realize how valuable your skills are to other potential employers."

Finally, Patty's sister devises a strategy for handling the clique. "Whatever they do," she advises, "don't react. Just stay neutral and focus on doing your job. The less they see that you're affected by their antics, the less pleasure they'll derive from harassing you."

This part of the plan is the most challenging for Patty to execute. But with practice and support, she's able to present a professional, neutral exterior to her mean girl colleagues. When she walks into the office, she greets each woman with, "Good morning," ignoring the fact that they may be snickering.

Should they give her misleading information, Patty acts as if it's an innocent mistake and goes on to correct the situation. Even when she suspects they're I.M.ing about her, she focuses her attention on the work at hand.

Eventually, the leader of the pack (the alpha mean girl) comes in and announces that her husband has been transferred overseas, and she's joining him. With her departure, the clique fractures. Patty still keeps a cool distance from the other mean girls, but acts courteously toward everyone in her department.

The Pack Attack—You're Attacked by a Group of Coworkers

What They Do

You're asked to join a female colleague for what seems like an innocent event:

- She asks you to accompany her to the conference room because she wants to show you something.
- She invites you to join her in the ladies' room.
- She suggests that you two meet for a drink after work.

When you follow her to the conference room, the ladies' room, or a bar for a drink, a surprise awaits you. Your colleague backs away, and you find yourself in the company of three or four women who clearly have a bone to pick with you. It suddenly dawns on you that you've been set up.

What transpires is a "pack attack." The women begin to bully and berate you. The subject matter could be the way you dress, the way you kiss up to the boss, or the fact that you're different from them. It could involve something work-related, but the attack is always personal.

How You Feel

You feel ambushed, violated, and emotionally beaten up. You may want to cry or lash out at them. You're shocked and unprepared. You feel vulnerable and unprotected.

Don't Go There

- Don't attack back—it won't get you anywhere and could worsen the situation.
- Don't cry or lash out—even though doing so will be very tempting.
- Don't run out of the room.

Go Here

Sometimes the best response is no response. Women who engage in pack attacks are trying to get a reaction out of you. They want to see you cry, yell, crumble, or run. Listen to them as best you can without responding. You may have to take deep breaths, count to 10, or silently tell yourself to hang on. Remember that the attack will die down if you don't respond. After a few minutes, excuse yourself by saying, "I've got to get back to work now." If they ask, "Don't you have anything to say?" simply respond, "No. I've got to get back to work."

Going Forward

Once you're out of the attack, you'll want to document it. Quickly record what happened. Jot down who the leader of the pack attack was, who led you into the attack, and what the group said to you. Once you've recorded this, you can report the incident to HR. If there is no HR department, report the incident to a safe person in authority—a man or woman who is capable of hearing about your experience and holding it in confidence.

Know that the leader of the pack is using her hostility toward you as a cover-up for her own incompetence and unhappiness. However, you may want to seek short-term counseling to recover from the trauma of being surprised and assaulted by a group of your peers. You don't want their mean behavior to cause you ongoing pain.

JUST BETWEEN US GIRLS

Most women who encounter groups of mean girls feel as if they're traveling back to the petty behavior of junior high and high school. Indeed, the behavior of mean girl cliques is inherently immature. Still, women continue to form packs throughout their lives. You may come across a group of grown-up mean girls at your church, in the PTA, at a social club, or within a charity.

Groups of mean girls are least powerful in organizations that are well managed, where the rules of conduct are clearly defined. You want to look for companies, associations, and causes where the leadership has a low tolerance for divisive behavior. Seek those places where professional conduct is encouraged and where performance is evaluated based on work product—not personal attacks.

CONCLUSION

Mean Girl Cheat Sheet and Parting Words

Here's a cheat sheet to help you stay professional as you deal with different kinds of mean girls in the workplace:

Meanest of the mean

What you need to remember — She's unable to see another person's point of view.

Very mean

What you need to remember — She's tough on the outside, but insecure on the inside.

Passively mean

What you need to remember — She's indirectly aggressive.

Doesn't mean to be mean

What you need to remember — She's extremely self-absorbed.

Doesn't know she's mean

What you need to remember — She's self-righteous and controlling.

Brings out your mean

What you need to remember — She's clueless.

Group mean

What you need to remember — They come in packs of two or three and are led by an alpha mean girl.

As you've discovered by reading this book, women are not all the same. They come to work with different interpersonal styles, a variety of psychological makeups, and a range of emotional baggage. And while we want to think that women should get along with one another naturally and easily, we have to realize that this is sometimes not the case. Instead, forming solid relationships is something that needs to be worked at.

Having read *Mean Girls at Work*, you've gained greater knowledge and practical tools for working with and supporting other women at work—no matter how different they are from you. If we can acknowledge that the workplace is naturally competitive, we can also strive to compete with one another in fair, productive, and professional ways.

Our hope is that if you've practiced mean behavior at work in the past, you can tame your inner "mean girl" and learn to get ahead without resorting to covert or indirect aggression toward other women. We also hope that if you've been the target of someone else's mean attacks, you've learned specific methods for protecting yourself professionally while not taking that mean girl's behavior to heart.

RESOURCES

How to Improve Your Marriage Without Talking About It, by Patricia Love and Steven Stosny (New York: Broadway Books, 2008).

In the Company of Women, by Pat Heim, Susan A. Murphy, and Susan K. Golant (New York: Tarcher/Putnam, 2001).

It's Always Personal, by Anne Kreamer (New York: Random House, 2011).

Tripping the Prom Queen: The Truth About Women and Rivalry, by Susan Shapiro Barash (New York: St. Martin's Press, 2006).

Why Men Never Remember and Women Never Forget, by Marianne Legato (Emmaus, PA: Rodale, 2005).

ABOUT THE AUTHORS

Katherine Crowley, a Harvard-trained psychotherapist, and **Kathi Elster**, a management consultant and executive coach, create the yin and yang of their company, K Squared Enterprises. Since 1989, they've combined their complementary expertise to develop a unique method for dealing with difficult people and challenging conditions at work. Their inside-out approach transforms the way businesses uncover and resolve their greatest interpersonal dilemmas.

Bestselling authors, educators, public speakers, executive coaches, and veteran consultants, Katherine and Kathi are seasoned guides in the area of professional fulfillment through self-awareness and self-management.

Kathi and Katherine have appeared on *Good Morning America*, CNN, *The Today Show, Good Day NY*, and numerous nationally syndicated radio shows. They've charmed audiences and led workshops at major universities, Fortune 100 companies, hospitals, and professional conferences around the country.

Together they have written *Working for You Isn't Working for Me*: *The Ultimate Guide to Managing Your Boss.* They are also the authors of the national bestseller *Working with You Is Killing Me: Freeing Yourself from Emotional Traps at Work.*